Special Urgency of Mercy

Why Sister Faustina?

by: Father George Kosicki, C.S.B.

Franciscan University Press, Steubenville, Ohio 43952
Marian Helpers, Stockbridge, Massachusetts
Divine Mercy Publications, Dublin, Ireland

Explanation of Cover Design

The source of mercy is the pierced Heart of Jesus on the Cross. The red rays represent the Blood of the Eucharist and the pale rays represent the water of Baptism and the Holy Spirit. The M represents Mary standing at the Cross as the Mother of Mercy, the Mediatrix of Mercy, our Merciful Mother (see John Paul II, *Rich in Mercy*, n. 9 and *Mother of the Redeemer*, n. 41).

The rays of mercy from the pierced Heart of Jesus descend upon Mary on the left, upon us as we stand on the right of the Cross as the beloved disciples, and upon the whole world.

> O BLOOD AND WATER WHICH GUSHED FORTH
> FROM THE HEART OF JESUS AS A FOUNT OF
> MERCY FOR US, I TRUST IN YOU! (Diary, n. 309)

Available in North America from:

Franciscan University Press, Franciscan University
of Steubenville, Steubenville, OH 43952

Marian Helpers, Stockbridge, MA 01263

Available in Ireland and Europe from:

Divine Mercy Publications, P.O. Box 2005,
Dublin 13, Ireland

Printed in the United States of America

ISBN: 0-940535-36-X

TABLE OF CONTENTS

Chapter   **Page**

Title

Table of Contents 3

Introduction 5

Dedication 9

1   Why Didn't Someone Tell Us? 11

2   So What's New About Sister Faustina? 17

3   Mercy, Mercy, Mercy! 21

4   Why is Sister Faustina So Special?.............25

5   How Do We Enter the Circle of Mercy,
        the Circle of Life? 29

6   How Does God Describe His Own Mercy? 33

7   Living in the Circle of Mercy..................39

8   What is So Special and Urgent About
        the Vessels of Mercy?.......................43

9   Sister Faustina: The Special Daughter
        of Mary, the Mother of Mercy 51

10   The Special Traits of the Spiritual
        Life of Sister Faustina 55

11   The Special Suffering of Sister Faustina 61

12   The Special Place of the Eucharist 67

13   Sister Faustina the Special Object of
        Satan's Hate 73

14   The Special Affinity of the Diary and
        Rich in Mercy 77

15   The Special Devotion of Sister Faustina
        to the Merciful Heart of Jesus 83

INTRODUCTION

This book is an urgent plea and exhortation to listen to the Lord's message of mercy in the way He presented it to us.

I began writing this book, because of the objection of a priest who said, "I can understand and preach God's mercy, but why Sister Faustina? The message of mercy is the gospel. I don't need private revelation and saints. That's old style spirituality." Another priest said, "I promote God's mercy but without reference to Sister Faustina, the gospel message is enough for me."

Still another reason that needs to be considered is the Second Coming of the Lord, because His coming again is integral to the message of Divine Mercy. The Lord made it clear to Sister Faustina this message of His mercy is in preparation for His coming. As Catholics, we have not faced up to the **fact** of the Lord's coming again. We all too easily explain it away by saying that He is always coming into our hearts. Thus, we pass off the serious study of it and leave the concern for the Lord's coming again to fundamentalist Christians. The burden of this book is that we hear the Lord's plea to prepare for His coming.

This present study was made possible because of the "thematic index" of the *Diary of Sister Faustina* compiled as a result of repeated readings of the **Diary**. The gathering together of related texts made it possible to see new dimensions that were always present but not developed. As a result of this study and writing, five special insights have enriched my understanding of the Lord's message of mercy: The special urgency of the message of Divine Mercy, the special role of Sister Faustina as God's choice, the Lord's plan that all glorify His mercy, the affinity of ideas between the *Diary of Sister Faustina* and the encyclical *Rich in Mercy*, and the special devotion of Sister Faustina to the Merciful Heart of Jesus.

The message of mercy has a **special urgency**. God has something to say to our generation. He wants us to hear Him, and act upon His word. He wants us to be prepared for His coming again. All too easily we use our free will to live our own lives according to our own plans and schedule, with no reference to God's plan and timing for our lives. We so easily claim freedom for ourselves and do not allow God His freedom to speak and direct our lives according to His will. God has spoken an urgent message. He wants it heard and we need to hear it. God has a right to speak. Do we have a right not to listen?

Sister Faustina is special and integral to God's message of mercy because God has decided to choose her as His own instrument. God chose His trumpet to announce His message rather than speak from a cloud with thunder and lightning. She is God's choice; she is His trumpet. We might like to choose our own instrument and play our own tune and march to a different rhythm, but God has made it clear that he is the concert master and composer of the score. If we don't know the score or don't like it and play our tune, we are really out of it. Woe to us if we do not recognize the Lord's coming, because we didn't know the day or the hour (Mt. 25:13).

The text of the gospel continues to ring in my mind:

> When the Son of Man comes, will He find any faith on the earth? (Lk. 18:8).

Has our generation become so "matured," so secularized, and so independent that it no longer needs the mercy of God announced to every generation?

> His mercy is on those who fear Him from generation to generation (Lk. 1:50).

In this generation, God has spoken His word of mercy again and in a new and urgent way through His special "Apostle and Secretary," Sister Faustina. Do we hear? Do we "fear" Him? Do we on earth have any faith?

God's overall and magnificent plan is that **all glorify His mercy**. This is the goal and purpose of His message of mercy:

That He might have mercy on all (Rom. 11:32).

This dimension of glorifying His mercy came into a new focus and awareness as a result of this writing. I am most thankful for this and appreciate all the more the first chapter of St. Paul's Letter to the Ephesians, which is a call to the praise of His glory:

That all might praise the glorious favor He has bestowed on us in His beloved (Eph. 1:6).

Sister Faustina wrote:

Glorifying your mercy is the **exclusive task of my life** (Diary 1242).

A special pleasure for me was to study the **"Affinity of ideas"** in *The Diary of Sister Faustina* and the encyclical of John Paul II *Rich in Mercy* as suggested by Cardinal Deskur. In studying the encyclical and in giving retreats based on it over the years, I noted at the side of the text, similarities with aspects of the Diary. It was only now, with a systematic study of both documents, that I came to see a profound link between the two in their themes and ideas:

Now is the time to turn to His mercy.

This study led me to a whole new area of the Diary: **The Merciful Heart of Jesus.** I discovered a gold mine, a treasure of infinite riches! In doing the thematic index of the Diary, I was aware of the many times Sister Faustina wrote of the rays of mercy coming from the Heart of Jesus and wondered why the Heart of Jesus was not dealt with more thoroughly in the study of the message. In the past, such writers as Father Ignatius Rozycki and Father Anthony Mruk, postulator of the cause of Sister Faustina, wrote with a concern to keep separate the devotion to the Sacred Heart and the veneration to the Divine Mercy. Their concern may have arisen from their desire to have the feast of Divine Mercy established and not be satisfied with response that "We have such a feast in the Solemnity of the Sacred Heart." But whatever their reasons and their arguments, I am not dealing with them here. In this book I am concerned about Sister Faustina's devotion to the Merciful Heart of Jesus as revealed to her by the Lord and as she practiced it. To my great delight and spiritual benefit I discovered that the devotion to the Merciful Heart of Jesus is an integral part of the message and unifies the message in the divine - human Heart of Jesus, in His very person. Devotion to the Merciful Heart of Jesus, as taught by Jesus and lived by Sister Faustina is for all of us a challenge to live in an intimate union with the Lord. Our hearts, purified and united with His Merciful Heart, will radiate His mercy to all. I am aware of Father Rubard Gilsdorf's review of the Diary of Sister Faustina, *Divine Mercy in My Soul* ending with the sweeping exhortation:

> For those who pray for a restoration of Roman-Catholicism in America and throughout the world, no greater work can be done than to disseminate this wondrous journal (*Homiletic and Pastoral Review*, December, 1988).

DEDICATION

To the Glory
of the Merciful Heart
of Jesus,

"That all might praise
the glorious favor
He has bestowed on us
in His beloved" (Eph. 1:6).

Chapter 1

WHY DIDN'T SOMEONE TELL US?

"Why didn't someone warn us?"

This will be the lament of many when the Lord Jesus comes again in His glorious manifestation.

"Why didn't someone tell us to get ready while we had time?"

This will be the complaint of so many when the shock of the reality strikes us.

But the Lord did warn us and told us to be ready when He was with us at the time of His first coming. For most the warning has lost its force of urgency as the twenty centuries rolled on. No longer are we waiting and praying, ready to greet the bridegroom on His return, because of dullness of mind and forgetfulness.

The **fact** of the Lord's coming again is our faith. It is in the Sacred Scriptures; we profess it in the Creed. We pray for it in every Lord's prayer and we express our longing for His coming in every celebration of the Mass. **That** He is coming is fact. But when and how He is coming is up to our

Heavenly Father. He knows and He can reveal His plan to whom He wishes, and when He wishes, in order to prepare for the glorious coming of Our Lord Jesus Christ.

The Lord has spoken through His prophets of our times to warn us, to exhort us to get ready that the time of His return is coming upon us. He has spoken through our Blessed Mother through a number of apparitions and locutions at Lourdes, Fatima, Medugorje and to Father Stefano Gobbi.

Very specifically He has also spoken to Sister Faustina Kowalska about His great merciful love being poured out in order to prepare for His coming. This is the time of His mercy, this is the day of mercy before His coming as just judge. Now is the time to turn to His mercy to repent from our sinful ways and to trust Him and be merciful.

Why didn't someone warn us? But, someone did warn us! In fact, someone is warning us right now. Let these very words before you be a warning that the Lord is coming very soon, that these are the days of His mercy in preparation for His coming again! Don't blame anyone for not telling you of the need to turn to His mercy, now, while it is time for His mercy.

Remember this day, today. Remember this warning: "He is coming soon!"

The message and warning given by Our Lord through Sister Faustina proclaim that His merciful love is so great that no sinner, no matter how wretched, need fear to come to His mercy. Our misery does not evoke His wrath, but only His tender mercies. The greater the sinner the more miserable the condition of the person; the greater the right they have to His mercy, in fact, the greatest right to His mercy. (Diary cf. 723)

Why have we not heard? Why have we not believed? Why have we not acted upon this word of God's mercy?

Because so few hear and believe the words of the prophets of the Lord. God has spoken and continues to speak, but we are deaf to God's revelations to our times and our hearts are hardened. We have neglected, explained away or simply forgotten the words of the Lord recorded for our benefit in the Sacred Scriptures about His coming again. And now when He speaks again the very "Truth and challenge of the gospel" (John Paul II, Fatima, May 13, 1982), Our hearts are hardened and our minds closed to the present light of truth.

Indeed, the Lord God does nothing without revealing His plan to His servants, the prophets.

The lion roars —
    who will not be afraid!
The Lord God speaks —
    who will not prophesy! (Amos 3:7-8).

The Lord God has indeed spoken through His prophets. Why have we not heard? For many reasons. One reason is that we believe the Church's teaching at the Second Vatican Council, and rightly so, that "we now await no further new public revelation before the glorious manifestation of our Lord Jesus Christ" (Vatican II, *Dei Verbuim* –4).

But this message of mercy is the **immediate preparation** for His glorious manifestation, so we can expect some "further new public revelation." This is the time of preparation, of a second "New Advent" as John Paul II repeatedly and clearly described in His Trilogy of encyclicals (*Redeemer of Man, Rich in Mercy,* and *Lord and Giver of Life*) and most fully in the *Mother of the Redeemer.* He announced this period of time before the millennium of the year 2001 as a special time of grace. He has a mystical sense about this special time. He exhorts us to prepare now.

I consider this millennium in my own way, as well, in the light of St. Peter's words:

> One day is as a thousand years and a thousand years are as a day (2Peter 3:8).

As we begin the third thousand years of Christ's first coming, we are entering the "Third day", the day of resurrection, the day of His glorious coming. Now is the time of immediate preparation for His glorious manifestation, so, we should expect some prophetic words of the Lord to warn and prepare us to greet Him on His coming again.

Some have difficulty accepting so called "private revelations", no matter what the source. In their freedom, they feel that the public revelation recorded in the Sacred Scriptures is enough for them and that is all they need for their salvation. That is true, but it's short sighted, because God also is free. God is free to speak to His children when and how He wants. And God has spoken to us and continues to speak to us because He has something to say to us! In our freedom, we cannot block God's freedom. God is freely and lovingly calling us, encouraging us, and warning us to come to His mercy now, while it is time for mercy. Others find difficulty with apparitions, visions, and locutions. Yet, our public revelation recorded in the Sacred Scriptures describes just such events: angels appearing at the annunciation to Mary, Joseph, to the Shepherds, to Jesus in the desert and in the garden, and to the woman at the empty tomb. The visions of Jesus at Tabor and Satan falling, of Peter and Joffa, Paul on the way to Damascus are part of our own public revelation. The locutions to Mary, Joseph, at the time of the annunciation, the words of the Father in regard to Jesus at His baptism and transfiguration, are recorded in the gospels. God chooses to use these very same means to speak to His children in this time of need.

The Lord God has spoken such a word of encouragement and warning to us in our times through His servant Sister Faustina:

You will prepare the world for my final coming (Diary 429).

And a similar word through our Blessed Mother:

I gave the Savior to the world; as for you, you have to speak to the world about His great mercy and prepare for His second coming (Diary 635).

The message of Our Lord to Sister Faustina is about His great mercy for all mankind. There is a great urgency about His message of mercy, because He wants no one to miss out on it when the day of justice comes:

Write down these words, My daughter, speak to the world about my mercy; let all mankind recognize my unfathomable mercy. It is a sign for end times; after it will come the day of justice. While there is still time, let them have recourse to the fount of my mercy; let them profit from the Blood and Water which gushed forth for them (Diary 848).

And this day of justice is coming upon us soon and so the loving warning to us now:

Secretary of my mercy, write, tell souls about this great mercy of mine, because the awful day, the day of my justice, is near (Diary 965).

"Why Sister Faustina?"

To answer our questions:

"Why didn't someone warn us?"

The Lord God sent Sister Faustina as His apostle (Diary 1142) with His message of mercy:

Come to my infinite mercy. Trust me. Be merciful. And so glorify my mercy.

We have been warned. Now we need to listen, trust and act! Now while it is time for mercy:

Mankind will not have peace until it turns with trust to my mercy (Diary 300).

Chapter 2

SO WHAT'S NEW ABOUT
SISTER FAUSTINA?

"We now await no further new public revelation before the glorious manifestation of our Lord Jesus Christ" (Dei Verbium #4, Vatican II).

The key issue in the revelation to Sister Faustina is that the message of mercy is given in order to be an immediate preparation for the coming of the Lord Jesus. So then, we can expect some new and urgent focus on "Truth and challenge of the gospel" (John Paul II, Fatima, May 13, 1982) in this time of a "new advent" (John Paul II).

The message of the first coming of our Lord is Jesus Christ himself. He is the message. He is Lord and Savior, Son of the Living God and Son of Mary by the Holy Spirit. In the words of the Second Vatican Council:

> God is with us to free us from the darkness of sin and death, and to raise us up to life eternal (Dei Verbum #4).

The message given through Sister Faustina is that "God

is Mercy itself" (cf. Diary 300, 1074) and wants all to come to His mercy, now while it is time for mercy. After this time of mercy, He will come in judgment (cf. **Diary** 848, 965). It is the "Truth and challenge of the gospel."

What is **new** in this message is not the content, but its **focus** on the "Truth and challenge of the gospel." The focus is urgent. It is now. It is strong and unique. It is teaching and a challenge to "eagerly await Him" (Heb. 9:28).

In these messages, there is an **urgent focus on NOW**. Now is the time for mercy; now is the time for salvation, before He comes in judgment. Sister Faustina recorded the Lord's words of urgency:

> While there is time, let (mankind) have recourse to the fount of my Mercy (Diary 848).

> The awful day, the day of my justice, is near (Diary 965).

> Before the Day of Justice I am sending the Day of Mercy (Diary 1588).

Now is the time for trust in the Lord, turning to His mercy with repentance, to be immersed in His mercy. Now is the time to plead for His mercy on us and on the whole world. Now is the time to be merciful like He is, merciful in word, prayer and deed. Now is the time to glorify His mercy.

The urgent focus is on **now**!

There is a **strong focus on holiness**, that is, our close union with the Lord God. Sister Faustina records for us the basic needs of a strong spiritual life: obedience to the will of God and to her spiritual director and superiors, the practice of humility as the foundation, frequent confession in the Sacrament of Reconciliation, Eucharistic worship, redemptive suffering for others, and a life consecrated to Mary, the Mother of God. Her diary is a magnificent teaching on the nature and practice of our life in intimacy with God. It is a strong call to holiness and to reflect and radiate the Lord's mercy (Diary 1074, 1695).

There is a **new focus on the vessels** that draw upon His mercy: a feast of Divine Mercy that would be like a new day of atonement (cf. Lev. 16 and Sirach 50) wiping out our past sins and punishment due to them (Diary 699), a new image of the merciful Savior that would be a vessel to draw His mercy and remind us to trust Him, a new prayer for mercy calling upon His passion in a Eucharistic offering in atonement for the sins of the world, and a daily time for immersing ourselves in His mercy, the 3:00 o'clock hour of His death on the cross. The focus of these new vessels is urgent and strong and clearly based on the public revelation of Jesus Christ recorded in the Sacred Scriptures. These new vessels are expressions of the one vessel of radical **trust** in Jesus Christ.

There is a **unique focus on God's mercy**. It is a focus on God's mercy rather than our own. Once we receive His mercy by trust in Him, that mercy reflects His, radiates and overflows like His own mercy. Only in and by **His** mercy can we live out the command of Jesus:

Be merciful, as your Father is merciful (Lk. 6:36).

Only in His mercy will we find any peace in our human condition. The word of our Lord to Sister Faustina places a unique focus on mercy:

Mankind will have no peace until it turns with trust to my mercy (Diary 300).

So now, we have received a new focus that is urgent, strong, and unique, as we await the glorious manifestation of Our Lord Jesus Christ (cf. Dei Verbum). Prepared and ready with trust in His mercy, we now eagerly await His coming again (cf. Heb. 9:28).

Chapter 3

MERCY, MERCY, MERCY!

We really need mercy in our human condition!

Mercy, mercy, mercy! is the cry that arises out of our hearts as we look around the world: Strife, violence, lust for power, wars, murders, avarice, abortions, drugs, famine, poverty, disasters and calamities and the list goes on and on. The human condition touches our own lives and families: rebellion, division, loss of faith, sickness and anxieties and, so too, this list goes on and on.

God sees and knows our human condition. In various ways the Lord described the condition of mankind to Sister Faustina (Diary 445). On top of the list is that we are sinners, full of sin, and in need of His mercy (Diary 50, 186, 687, 699, 723, 1059, 1146, 1160, 1275, 1320, 1396, 1520, 1521, 1541, 1572, 1665, 1666, 1728, 1784). We are miserable (Diary 723, 1273, 1602, 1777, 1798), lost (Diary 965, 998, 1397) separated by an abyss (Diary 512, 1576), aching (Diary 1074, 1588), and in need of salvation (Diary 1182, 1777, 1452, 1784). And He goes on to say that in this time prior to the Day of Judgment (Diary 83, 848) that we are distressed (Diary 1541), distrustful (Diary 50, 177, 379, 1074, 1076, 1160), lukewarm (Diary 341, 1228, 1447, 1448, 1577), fainting with lack of peace (Diary 300, 699). And to top off the list we are attacked by the enemy, Satan and His cohorts (Diary 378, 723, 1516, 1540).

The word of Our Lord to Sister Faustina during a vision of His passion applies to us: "Look and see the human race in its present condition" (Diary 445).

We really do need God's mercy to bring us His salvation. There is no other salvation for mankind than the mercy of our Lord Jesus Christ.

And the mercy of God is available for all who come to Him for mercy. There is no limit to His mercy if we fulfill our part. Our part is to **receive** the gift of His mercy He offers us. It is pure gift, but it must be received, allowed to work a change in us in order that we may pass on this mercy to Him in thanksgiving and praise, and to others, in our words, prayer and deeds. "Be merciful as your Father is merciful" (Lk. 6:36).

The only way mankind will find salvation and peace in this human condition is to turn with trust to God's mercy (cf. Diary 300, 699). There is no other salvation, there will be no other, and there can be no other. Mercy is our salvation.

And this mercy is so great that there is no human condition, individually, or globally that cannot be saved by His mercy. It is God's plan and desire "to have mercy on all" (Rom. 11:32). His mercy is greater than all evil, greater than all sin and greater than death itself (cf. John Paul II, Dives in Misericordia, #15).

The merciful Lord desires that we receive His mercy, use it, and give it away! He will not force us to receive His mercy. He so respects our free will that He asks us to receive His mercy. The Scripture texts that illustrate this best for me is the message of the Church at Laodicea: "Here I stand, knocking at the door. If anyone hears me calling and opens the door, I will enter His house and have supper with Him, and

He with me. I will give the victor the right to sit with me on my throne" (Rev. 3:20-21). Jesus stands at the door of my heart and knocks! He is waiting for me to open up my heart to Him. He is waiting. That is real humility.

In our human condition, we are in an enormous debt to God (Diary 1226, 1316). Our national debt is like pennies compared to our debt to Him. Out of His mercy He created us and continues to sustain us and then more than that, He redeemed us by a flood of mercy while yet sinners (cf. Rom. 5:8). What has increased our debt so dramatically is that we have not received His mercy with trust. We continue to be indifferent (Diary 341), and lukewarm (Diary 1228), and continue sinning and living as though there were no God.

And still God in His loving mercy is ready, willing, and able to flood us with His mercy, if we but open our hearts to Him. Our Lord told Sister Faustina:

> How very much I desire the salvation of souls! I want to pour out my divine life into human souls and to sanctify them, **if only** they were willing to accept my grace. The greatest sinners would achieve great sanctity, **if only** they would trust in my mercy... (Diary 1784).

"**If only**...", if only they were willing, if only they would trust, if only they would accept, if only they would surrender to His merciful love and open the door of their hearts to Him, and if only they knew the gift of God (cf. Jn. 4:10). "If only" is the very touch point of man and God—if only man would use his free will to freely respond and cooperate with God's will and not his own.

Man in his human condition deserves God's justice, but God in His condition wants to pour out His mercy. A priest friend of mine described this difference between justice and mercy in terms of God's love for us. **Justice** is God's love poured out on us for what we deserve. **Mercy** is God's love poured out on us for what we don't deserve!

In our human condition we don't deserve anything but "Tough Love", His justice. But God's plan and desire is to pour out His love on us because in no way do we deserve it, in no way can we earn it. That is God's mercy!

That is why in our human condition we cry. "Mercy, Mercy, Mercy, Jesus, have mercy on us and on the whole world" (cf. Diary 475, 476).

Chapter 4

WHY IS SISTER FAUSTINA SO SPECIAL?

Because **God chose her**!

A simple answer but it is the real and true answer. This book is an attempt to answer the question of what makes Sister Faustina so special.

There are a number of **special** features about the life and mission of Sister Faustina that makes her special. They all are based on the fact that God decided to **choose** her (Diary 400, 417, 1605, 1700) as a special instrument of revealing His merciful love in preparation for His coming again. It all started with His choice of her.

Let us look at those various special features that stand out in her diary in order to appreciate and, hopefully, to act more fully in response to the message of mercy.

Special because God called her by special titles

The Lord called Sister Faustina by some **special titles** that described her role in this message of mercy. He called her

witness of His mercy (Diary 164, 400, 417, 689, 699, 848, 1074) by her life, **apostle** of His mercy proclaiming His mercy to all (Diary 1142, 1588), and **secretary** of His mercy by writing down everything He said about His mercy for the sake of others (Diary 965, 1273, 1275, 1605, 1784). He also referred to her as His **instrument** (Diary 645), **dispenser** (Diary 31, 580), **mediator** and **intercessor** of His mercy (Diary 438, 441, 599). He topped the list of special titles by calling her a **Saint** (Diary 1571, 1650).

Special because God called her to a special union with Him

The Lord God called Sister Faustina to a **unique union** with Him (Diary 512, 587, 603,707, 718, 969, 1109, 1546, 1576, 1693), to be His dwelling place (Diary 167, 238, 346, 431, 451, 911) to be His delight (Diary 27, 137, 164, 339, 346, 451), as His spouse (Diary 158, 239, 534), and as His living reflection (Diary 1446). In this unique union, she was gifted as a special daughter of Mary (Diary 1414) with a gift of purity (Diary 40).

The purpose of this special and unique union with the Lord was to make her an apt missioner of His message of mercy.

Special because of her God-given mission

The Lord God gave Sister Faustina a special mission to **prepare for His second coming** (Diary 429, 635 [spoken by Mary], 1732). She was to carry out this mission by **proclaiming His mercy to all** (Diary 50, 300, 301, 378, 379, 570, 655, 848, 1074, 1142, 1190, 1396, 1448, 1516, 1666, 1728), especially to sinners, and to tell priests to proclaim His mercy (Diary 50, 177, 570, 687, 1521). She was commissioned to **write** about His mercy for the sake of others (Diary 83, 570, 675, 848, 895, 1074, 1142, 1146, 1160, 1182, 1273, 1317, 1448, 1540, 1541, 1567, 1665, 1667, 1728, 1739, 1784). She was to **spread devotion** to His Divine Mercy (Diary 998, 1074, 1075, 1540, 1667). She was to make known His desire for a feast of Divine Mercy, for an image of the merciful Savior, for the Chaplet of Divine Mercy, and for the 3:00 o'clock remembrance, all of which are vessels to draw upon His mercy.

In a special way she was commissioned to **win souls'** cooperation with His mercy (Diary 1690). She was to win souls by her **prayer**, appealing to His mercy (Diary 570, 1146, 1155, 1160, 1182, 1521, 1572, 1578, 1690), even pleading (Diary 482, 570, 1216, 1218, 1220, 1224, 1226, 1228), especially for sinners (Diary 186, 206, 1397), saying the Chaplet of Divine Mercy unceasingly (Diary 687). She was also to win souls by her **sacrifice of suffering** as a victim of love (Diary 726, 923, 955) for others (Diary 67, 723, 895, 1612, 1645) with Christ (Diary 151, 310, 348, 675), but only with her consent (Diary 135, 136, 308, 309, 1264). Also, she was to win souls by **encouraging** others to trust in His mercy (Diary 1182, 1452, 1540, 1690).

To carry out this mission of mercy she was gifted with a **profound understanding** of His mercy (Diary 180, 438, 835, 873, 1456, 1506, 1572) and a special **share in His mercy** in order to be always merciful as the Lord (Diary 1695, 1777) and in order to be strong in spiritual warfare (Diary 145, 1760).

Our Lord also commissioned Sister Faustina to **distribute His mercy in this life** (Diary 31, 438, 580, 1695), mediating His mercy (Diary 438, 1777). For her sake Jesus granted many graces (Diary 383), blessing the earth (Diary 39, 431, 719, 1061, 1078, 1732) and by restraining the hand of justice (Diary 198, 431, 1722).

This special mission of mercy is to **continue in heaven** (Diary 281, 483, 1209).

But there is still more that is special about Sister Faustina.

Special because of her life

Sister Faustina lived a life of humility and obedience. The

will of God made known through her spiritual directors and superiors, were her only will. Her life was one of complete trust in God's mercy, a life dedicated to the Holy Eucharist, as her full name indicates, Sister Maria Faustina of the Blessed Sacrament, and life consecrated to Mary, the Mother of God, as a special daughter.

Her whole life and mission was a glorification of God's mercy.

Her life was special, because she so perfectly fulfilled the beatitude of mercy: "Blessed are the merciful for they shall obtain mercy" (Mt. 5:7), the command "Be merciful as your Father is merciful" (Lk. 6:36), the exhortation "Learn of me because I am meek and humble of heart" (Mt. 11:29), and the prayer of Jesus in the garden "Not My will but yours be done" (Lk. 22:42). More will be developed on these topics in following chapters.

Yes, Sister Faustina is special! Because God chose her to be His special instrument to reveal His mercy to the world now, while it is time for mercy, now while it is time of preparation for His coming again.

Chapter 5

HOW DO WE ENTER THE
CIRCLE OF MERCY,
THE CIRCLE OF LIFE?

Mercy is the circle of life. The outpouring of God's mercy when it is totally received and given is the circle of life. It reflects the great circle of love within the life of the most Holy Trinity. The Father totally gives His all to His Son and the Son receives and returns the gift of all in the Holy Spirit. Pope Paul VI described this circle as "The secret of life of the Trinity: the Father is seen here as the one who gives Himself to the Son, without reserve and without ceasing, in a burst of joyful generosity, and the Son is seen as He gives Himself in the same way to the Father in a burst of joyful gratitude in the Holy Spirit. All who believe in Christ are called to share this joy" (**Gaudete in Domino**, 1975).

All of us are called to share in this joy, this circle of mercy and love. This is eternal life. It is God's will and plan that we all share in this joy and life (cf. Jn. 17:13). "I have come that they may live and have life to the full" (Jn. 10:10).

How do we enter this circle of mercy and life? By totally

receiving and totally giving His mercy, or by the reverse, by totally giving and so receiving. "Blessed are the merciful for they shall obtain mercy" (Mt. 5:7). It is a great circle, and we can enter the circle at any point in a number of ways. A number of doors are opened for us to enter as we respond to God's initial and continuous outpouring of His merciful love.

A number of the doors that we can enter are described for us in the diary of Sister Faustina in the words of Jesus. Any one of them will bring us into this vibrant and radiant circle of mercy and life. On the top of the list is **TRUST** (Diary 300, 420, 570, 687, 723, 742, 1059, 1182, 1273, 1452, 1488, 1520, 1541, 1578, 1602, 1777, 1784). Trust in the Lord is the first act of mercy. By trust, we receive His mercy and allow it to change us. Trust is a radical faith in God as Lord of all and Savior of the Lord; it is a joyful hope in what He has prepared for us and it is a firm and perserving love for God and neighbor. By trust, we enter the circle of mercy and life.

To enter the circle of mercy and life we can imitate the special mission of Sister Faustina. As we carry out the commission to Sister Faustina we too become witnesses and apostles of His Divine Mercy. Each commission we carry out opens a door into the circle of mercy (please refer to the Diary references in the Chapter "Why is Sister Faustina so special?").

Like Sister Faustina we too can proclaim God's infinite mercy, telling all to come to His mercy, to encourage all, especially sinners, to trust in His mercy. We too can pray and beg for God's mercy, appealing for it, and immersing all in it. We can be apostles and witnesses of His great mercy by the lives we live, being merciful to others as He is and so radiating and reflecting His mercy. We can invite ourselves to Christ in Holy Communion. In union with Him, we too can offer our sufferings as a loving sacrifice for others. We too can be cleansed in the "tribunal of mercy", the sacrament of reconciliation. As we accept His graces and mercy and use them, we too can grow in a special union with Him, experiencing an ever deeper knowledge of Him.

Like Sister Faustina we too can spread devotion to the Divine Mercy by the special vessels of trust and prayer He revealed to her. We can celebrate the feast of mercy, venerate the image of the merciful Savior, pray the chaplet, and remember the death of the Lord at 3:00 o'clock.

There is still another grand door in which to enter the circle of mercy and life. It is jeweled and precious. It is the door that unites us with our Blessed Mother, the angels and saints at the throne of God:

The door of **glorifying** His mercy!

Each of the other doors we described have as their purpose and goal the glory of God. But glorifying His mercy directly and specifically is a unique door into His radiant life.

Our Lord made it very clear to Sister Faustina that He wants His mercy glorified:

> Give praise and glory to this mercy of mine (Diary 206).

> I demand that the people revere My mercy (Diary 742).

> If they will not adore My mercy they shall perish (Diary 965).

> I desire that My mercy be worshiped (Diary 998).

> At three o'clock immerse yourself in My mercy, adore and glorify it, invoke its omnipotence... I claim veneration for My mercy from every creature (Diary 1572).

Then the Lord also described the **ways** we can glorify His mercy:

> When a sinner turns to My mercy He gives glory...(Diary 378).

> To priests who proclaim and extol My mercy, I will give wondrous powers (Diary 1521).

To those who glorify My mercy, spread its worship, encourage trust, I will protect at death (Diary 1540).

Beg for sinners that they may glorify My mercy (Diary 1160).

Make the novena so that every soul will glorify My mercy (Diary 1059).

And to those who glorify His mercy the Lord promises through Sister Faustina:

I will deal according to My infinite mercy at the hours of their death (Diary 379).

Their names are written in this book [of life] (Diary 689).

Glorifying the mercy of God was the very reason and purpose of Sister Faustina's life (Diary 835, 1604, 1242). She glorified God's mercy in all her words, deeds and prayers. More beautifully she praised the mercy of God in her litany of mercy (Diary 949).

How beautifully St. Paul glorifies the mercy of God after he says that God's plan and desire is to "have mercy on all."

How deep are the riches and wisdom and the knowledge of God!... From Him and through Him and for Him all things are. To Him be **glory** forever. Amen (Rom. 11:32-36).

Sister Faustina records St. Paul's praise of God's glory in her diary (Diary 1604).

How shall we enter the great circle of mercy and life? By glorifying God's mercy in all our words, prayers and deeds. By receiving His mercy with trust and being merciful to others.

Glory be to your infinite, holy and living mercy now and forever.

Chapter 6

HOW DOES GOD DESCRIBE HIS OWN MERCY?

"I am mercy itself" (Diary 281, 300, 1074, 1148, 1273, 1739, 1777).

That's how God describes His mercy to Sister Faustina. John tells us that "God is love" (1 Jn. 4:16). The two descriptions complement each other. God in Himself is love and when that love is poured out in creation, redemption, and sanctification, it is mercy. Mercy is God's love poured out. It is love's second name (John Paul II *Dives In Misericordia*).

The Lord delights in the title "Mercy" (Diary 300), because it so beautifully describes who He is and how He longs to pour out His mercy on us. He also calls Himself the "King of Mercy" (Diary 83, 88), and the merciful Savior (Diary 1075, 1541), and he refers to His merciful Heart (e.g. Diary 177, 1074, 1152, 1447, 1520, 1588, 1602, 1682, 1689, 1728, 1739, 1777). But those titles give only a hint of His great desire to be merciful.

Throughout her diary, Sister Faustina records for us the words of the Lord describing this great desire He has to share

His mercy with souls. He yearns for souls (Diary 206, 1182, 1521, 1784) and keeps pouring out His mercy (Diary 50, 177, 699, 703, 1074, 1159, 1190, 1689, 1784), clamoring to be spent (Diary 177) like a burning flame within Him (Diary 50, 177, 186, 1074, 1190, 1521). His desire is greatest for sinners (Diary 206, 378, 723, 1146, 1275, 1665, 1739, 1784), especially for the miserable (Diary 723, 1182, 1273, 1541). His compassion overflows (Diary 1148, 1190, 1777), with arms open and waiting (Diary 206, 1541, 1728, 1777). He excludes no one (Diary 1076, 1182, 1728), and asks only for trust, unlimited trust (see texts of trust). His mercy defends us (Diary 1516), especially at the hour of death (Diary 378, 379, 754, 1075, 1540). But the description of His desire to spend His mercy on us is not enough, there is more.

The Lord also describes the very nature of His mercy, but there is no adequate language for it. It is ineffable (Diary 359) and cannot be imagined or conceived with our minds (Diary 699, 1142). So, the Lord uses a variety of adjectives and images to give us some appreciation of the magnificence of His mercy. He describes it like an ocean (Diary 699, 718, 1209, 1210, 1214, 1216, 1218, 1273, 1520) with bottomless depth (Diary 88, 420, 570, 699, 811, 848, 1059, 1142, 1146, 1182, 1190, 1517, 1521, 1777), with no limits and inexhaustible (Diary 50, 718, 1273) like a great abyss (Diary 180, 206, 1226, 1228, 1541, 1576, 1777). It is infinite (Diary 378, 687, 689); it is great (Diary 300, 378, 379, 635, 699, 965, 1396).

He also uses the image of the fountain echoing the image of John's gospel, "Let anyone who thirsts come to me and drink... Rivers of living water with flow from within Him" (Jn. 7:37-38). This fountain of mercy (Diary 187, 327, 848, 1075, 1182, 1209, 1488, 1520, 1602, 1777), is opened wide for us (Diary 1146, 1159, 1182, 1520, 1572). In a wonderful way, the Lord describes His pierced side on the cross from which gushed forth blood and water as a fount of mercy (Diary 187).

This great mercy of our Lord is like an ocean and like a fountain, and yet, it is tender (Diary 420, 699, 811, 848). It is the greatest of His attributes (Diary 180, 301). It is His love poured out on us. It is confirmed in every work, culminating in forgiveness (Diary 723).

The Lord also portrayed His mercy visually to Sister Faustina as rays of red and pale light coming from His pierced side, as rays from the fount of mercy (Diary 1309). These rays of His merciful love (Diary 370) issued from the very depths of His tender mercy when His agonizing heart was opened with a lance on the cross (Diary 299). Not only did Sister Faustina see these rays of mercy from the area of the heart of Jesus as depicted in the image of the merciful Savior, but on a number of occasions she saw these same two rays emanating from the Eucharist (Diary 336, 344, 370, 420, 441, 657, 1046), from His Sacred Heart (Diary 177, 414, 1559, 1565, 1796), and at times the rays covered the whole world (Diary 87, 441, 1796).

Jesus exhorts us to live in the shelter of these rays of mercy shielded from the just hand of God and His wrath (Diary 299).

Is it any wonder that God's mercy is praised by the souls in heaven (Diary 753) and glorified by St. Paul in His canticle of mercy:

> Oh, the depth of the riches and wisdom and knowledge of God! How inscrutable are His judgments and how unsearchable His ways! ... For from Him and through Him and for Him are all things. To Him be glory forever. Amen. (Rom. 11:30-36).

As an example of the description of God's mercy and His great desire for the souls of sinners, the dialogue of the merciful God with a sinful Soul stands out as a prime example:

> Jesus: Be not afraid of your Savior, O sinful soul. I make the first move to come to you, for I know that

by yourself you are unable to lift yourself to me. Child, do not run away from your Father; be willing to talk openly with your God of mercy who wants to speak words of pardon and lavish His graces on you. How dear your soul is to Me! I have inscribed your name upon My hand; you are engraved as a deep wound in My Heart.

Soul: Lord, I hear your voice calling me to turn back from the path of sin, but I have neither the strength nor the courage to do so.

Jesus: I am your strength, I will help you in the struggle.

Soul: Lord, I recognize your holiness, and I fear You.

Jesus: My child, do you fear the God of mercy? My holiness does not prevent Me from being merciful. Behold, for you I have established a throne of mercy on earth - the tabernacle - and from this throne I desire to enter into your heart. I am not surrounded by a retinue or guards. You can come to me at any moment, at any time; I want to speak to you and desire to grant you grace.

Soul: Lord, I doubt that You will pardon my numerous sins; my misery fills me with fright.

Jesus: My mercy is greater than your sins and those of the entire world. Who can measure the extent of my goodness? For you I descended from heaven to earth; for you I allowed myself to be nailed to the cross; for you I let my Sacred Heart be pierced with a lance, thus opening wide the source of mercy for you. Come, then, with trust to draw graces from this fountain. I never reject a contrite heart. Your misery has disappeared in the depths of My mercy. Do not argue with Me about your wretchedness. You will give me pleasure if you hand over to me all your troubles and griefs. I shall heap upon you the treasures of My grace.

Soul: You have conquered, O Lord, my stony heart with Your goodness. In trust and humility I approach the tribunal of Your mercy, where You yourself absolve me by the hand of your representative. O Lord, I feel Your grace and Your peace filling my poor soul. I feel overwhelmed by Your mercy, O Lord. You forgive me, which is more than I dared to hope for or could imagine. Your goodness surpasses all my desires. And now, filled with gratitude for so many graces, I invite You to my heart. I wandered, like a prodigal child gone astray; but you did not cease to be my Father. Increase Your mercy toward me, for You see how weak I am.

Jesus: Child, speak no more of your misery; it is already forgotten. Listen, My child, to what I desire to tell you. Come close to My wounds and draw from the Fountain of Life whatever your heart desires. Drink copiously from the Fountain of Life and you will not weary on your journey. Look at the splendors of My mercy and do not fear the enemies of your salvation. Glorify My mercy (Diary 1485).

The Conversation of the merciful God with a Despairing Soul (Diary 1486), with a Suffering Soul (Diary 1487), with a soul striving after perfection (Diary 1488), and with a Perfect Soul (Diary 1489) are a marvelous set of teachings on God's mercy. They could be printed as a pamphlet on the interior life for frequent reading and reflection by all of us.

Chapter 7

LIVING IN THE CIRCLE OF MERCY

How do we live in this great circle of mercy? How do we remain under the shelter of the two rays of His mercy?

Sister Faustina records for us her way of living in God's mercy and radiance. "I remain with Him in the depths of my heart. It is in my own soul that I most easily find God." (Diary 903) She abided constantly with her Beloved (see Diary 454, 582 and Jn. 15:4), and nothing exterior hindered her union with God. Our Lord spoke about the importance of this union with Him in our hearts:

> Oh, if souls would only want to listen to My voice when I am speaking in the depths of their hearts, they would reach the peak of holiness in a short time (Diary 584).

Sister Faustina lived in great intimacy with the Lord, listening to Him (Diary 584) talking to Him (Diary 581, 797, 1692), loving Him, and seeking to do His will always. She gave herself to Him in complete and radical trust that she could be an instrument and channel of His mercy. Her whole diary is a record of this intimacy with the Lord. Her life could be capsulized in her trust and mercy by which she glorified the Lord (for more see the Chapter on the Devotion to the MHJ).

We too are called and challenged to live a life of **trust** and **mercy** by which we **glorify** the Lord. The revelations to Sister Faustina give us concrete ways to live and grow in this intimate union with God, to live in this circle of love. Let us consider two of the principle ones:

The **image** of the merciful Savior with the inscription "Jesus I trust in You!" and the **Chaplet** of Divine Mercy as a way of exercising mercy for others.

The **image** of the merciful Savior is a visual reminder of His presence to us in our hearts. He blesses us, irradiates us with His rays of mercy, shielding us and reminding us to express our trust in Him over and over again: "Jesus, I trust in you!" Our trust in Jesus is our continual and complete "yes" to Him. By our trust, we express by our lives of faith in Him, our love for Him, our longing for Him, and our desire to serve Him. By our trust in Jesus, we glorify Him and please Him greatly. Each time we see the image, we venerate the Lord by professing with our heart, "Jesus, I trust in You!" This expression of trust fans into flame our awareness of God's presence within our hearts (see 2 Tim. 1:6). This cry of "Jesus, I trust in You." can be on our lips and hearts through the day and night as a way of responding to the Lord's presence in our hearts. It is a powerful way to live in the circle of mercy.

The image can be displayed in an honorable place in our homes and also in our places of work. We can carry a smaller card of the image with us as a reminder of God's abiding presence. What about gluing a small image onto the dash board of your car? A great prayer place!

The **Chaplet** of Divine Mercy is a way of exercising mercy by praying for ourselves and for the whole world. The exercise of mercy toward others is commanded by our Lord (see Lk. 6:36) and explained to Sister Faustina:

> ...I demand from you deeds of mercy, which are to arise out of love for Me. You are to show mercy to your neighbors always and everywhere. You must not shrink from this or try to excuse or absolve yourself from it. I am giving you three ways of exercising mercy toward your neighbor: The first - by deed, the second - by word, the third - by prayer. In these three degrees is contained the fullness of mercy, and it is an unquestionable proof of love for Me. By this means a soul glorifies and pays reverence to My mercy (Diary 742).

Our Lord taught Sister Faustina the lesson of Mary at His feet who had chosen the better part (Lk. 10:42) and asked of her to exercise *"mercy in spirit"* by praying for others and offering loving sacrifices for them (see "Why is Sister Faustina so special?"). This challenge and request is to us as well:

> Daughter, I need sacrifice lovingly accomplished, because that alone has meaning for me. Enormous indeed are the debts of the world which are due to me; pure souls can pay them by their sacrifice, exercising **mercy in Spirit** (Diary 1316).

The Lord goes on to point out that **mercy in Spirit** can always and everywhere be exercised:

> ... Write this for the many souls who are often worried because they do not have the material means with which to carry out an act of mercy. Yet **spiritual mercy**, which requires neither permissions nor storehouses, is much more meritorious and is within the grasp of every soul. If a soul does not exercise mercy somehow or other, it will not obtain My mercy on the day of judgment. Oh, if only souls knew how to gather eternal treasure for themselves they would

not be judged, for they would forestall My judgment with their mercy (Diary 1317).

The Chaplet of Divine Mercy is a concrete way of exercising "mercy in Spirit". It is a loving offering of the sacrifice of our Lord Jesus Christ in atonement for our sins and those of the whole world. It is a pleading for mercy on all. It is a way "to gather eternal treasures". Our Lord asked Sister Faustina to pray the Chaplet "unceasingly" (Diary 687) and said that "Through the Chaplet you will obtain everything, if what you ask will be compatible with My will" (Diary 1731).

A short form of the Chaplet is the cry "Jesus, Mercy!" (see e.g. Diary 118, 119, 869). The plea for God's mercy in every situation of need that we encounter is a way of "exercising mercy in Spirit". It goes to the source of mercy, Jesus, and asks for the only answer to our need, His mercy. The prayer "Jesus, mercy" is always available to us, so that, we may immerse the present situation or person in the sea of His merciful love.

How do we live in the circle of mercy? By living in the presence of mercy Itself who is present in our heart. By fanning into a flame His radiant presence by expressing our trust in Him: "Jesus, I trust in you." By expressing this trust with our hearts and lips. And by exercising mercy in spirit by pleading mercy on us and on the whole world: "Jesus, mercy."

"Jesus, I trust in you" and "Jesus, Mercy", prayed without ceasing from the heart is a succinct summary of the spiritual life. These two prayers are the experience of the total giving and receiving of the inner life of the Holy Trinity. We ask for His mercy and receive it with trust that we may live in that intimacy of His radiant mercy.

"Jesus, I trust in you."
"Jesus, Mercy!"

Chapter 8

WHAT IS SO SPECIAL AND URGENT ABOUT THE VESSELS OF MERCY?

The vessels of mercy are special because God designed them and described them to Sister Faustina and asked that they be used to draw upon His mercy. To each of them: the Feast of Divine Mercy, the Image of Divine Mercy, the Chaplet of Divine Mercy, the three o'clock Hour of Mercy, and the Novena before the Feast of Divine Mercy, the Lord attached promises of special graces. Because they are of the Lord's initiative and His urging, they are special and have an urgency about them as means of preparing for His coming.

The Feast of Divine Mercy

The Feast of Divine Mercy reflects the Old Testament feast of the Day of Atonement when all sin and debts were wiped away (see Lv. 16 and Sirach 50). Our Lord asked that we celebrate His mercy on the Sunday after Easter with the reception of Holy Communion and prepare for it with the sacrament of reconciliation and a novena. Priests are to preach on His mercy, the image is to blessed, and everyone is to perform some act of Mercy (Diary 299, 300, 699, 796) on that day.

This feast emerged from the very depth of the Lord's tender mercy (Diary 699) and so the flood gates of His Divine Mercy are open to all who come to celebrate the feast. No one should fear to approach Him, because he wants to wipe away all sin and punishment due to them (Diary 699). What a promise!

"Complete forgiveness of sins and punishment!" (Diary 699). How we need this grace! A clean slate to start over again, like a second Baptism. There is so much sin in the world and our debt to God is so enormous (Diary 1226, 1316) that we need a sovereign act of God's mercy like this feast to rescue us.

This feast is God's plan for a sovereign act of mercy on all. He points out that the feast which expresses our trust in Him, is our last hope, the last plank or lifesaver, for our salvation (Diary 965, 998). His heart rejoices in this feast and wants it for the consolation of the world (Diary 1517). He concludes His explanations of the feast with the warning: "Mankind will have no peace until it turns with trust to My mercy" (Diary 300, 699).

The Feast of Divine Mercy is so special and urgent, because it is God's plan of mercy for our human condition of misery. There is no other chance for our peace and salvation than by turning with trust to His mercy.

How we need this feast!

The Image of the Merciful Savior

"Paint an image according to the pattern you see" (Diary 47) echoes the command Our Lord gave to Moses in building the tabernacle of the Old Testament: "See that you make everything according to the pattern shown you on the mountain [Sinai]" (Heb 8:5 and Ex. 25:40). Moses followed the model of what he saw in heaven while on Mount Sinai and built on earth the tabernacle of the Lord. Sister Faustina saw the Lord Jesus coming toward her with His hand raised in blessing, dressed in a white robe, with large red and pale rays emanating from the area of His heart, looking at us as from the cross (Diary 47, 326).

The reality she saw, she tried to have painted, but the artist couldn't capture the beauty of the model, Jesus radiant and victorious. The beauty and greatness of this image of Jesus, however, is not in the paint but in His grace (cf. Diary 313).

The fact that Jesus modeled and asked for this image to be painted is unique. It places this image in the class of those not painted by human hands, such as the face of Christ in the Byzantine Icon under that title, or the face of Christ in the shroud of Turin.

The promises Our Lord obtained for those who venerate of His image depicted as the merciful Savior are very special: The soul will not perish, it will be victorious over its enemies here on earth and especially at the hour of death, the Lord will defend it as His own glory (Diary 48). The rays shield souls who dwell in their shelter from the wrath of the Father and the just hand of God will not lay hold of them (Diary 299).

In a sweeping description of this image He tells Sister Faustina:"I am offering people a vessel with which they are to keep coming for graces to the fountain of mercy. That vessel is the image with the signature: "Jesus, I trust in you" (Diary 327).

The image of the merciful Savior was so special to Sister Faustina that she introduced her first notebook of her Diary with a poem about the image:

> O Eternal Love, you command your Sacred Image
> to be painted and reveal to us the inconceivable fount
> of mercy.
>
> You bless whoever approaches your rays.
>
> And a soul all black will turn into snow... (Diary 1).

How should we venerate this image? By having it blessed and hung in our homes and even carried with us in order to remind us to draw mercy from the fount of mercy, to trust Him, and to do works of mercy (Diary 742).

> By means of this image I shall grant many graces to souls (Diary 742).

The Image of Divine Mercy really is special, because the Lord has made it so.

The Chaplet of Divine Mercy

The Chaplet of Divine Mercy is special, because the Lord designed it as a special vessel of grace and He Himself taught it to Sister Faustina. It is a priestly and Eucharistic prayer for mercy, for all in need of mercy, and can be said at anytime.

So, our Lord's promises are special for those who pray the Chaplet:

> Oh what great graces I will grant to souls who say this Chaplet: the very depths of My tender mercy are stirred for the sake of those who say the Chaplet (Diary 848).

> My daughter, encourage souls to say the Chaplet which I have given to you. It pleases me to grant everything they ask of me by saying the Chaplet (Diary 1541) ... Through the Chaplet you will obtain everything, if what you ask for will be compatible with My will (Diary 1731).

> When hardened sinners say it, I will fill their souls with peace, and the hour of their death will be a happy one... (Diary 1541).

> Write that when they say this Chaplet in the presence of the dying, I will stand between My Father and the dying person, not as the just Judge but as

the merciful Savior (Diary 1541) and a similar promise in (Diary 811), "The souls that will say this Chaplet will be embraced by My mercy during their lifetime and especially at the hour of their death" (Diary 754).

This promise is made to priests: "Priests will recommend the Chaplet to sinners as their last hope of salvation. Even if there were a sinner most hardened, if he were to recite this Chaplet only once, he would receive grace from My infinite mercy. **I desire that the whole world know My infinite mercy. I desire to grant unimaginable graces to those souls who trust in My mercy (Diary 687).**

This is God's desire and plan! That we trust in His mercy, that we draw unimaginable graces from His mercy, and that the whole world know His infinite mercy.

The vessel, the instrument, that God has given us to remind us to trust in Him and to draw upon His graces and mercies is His Chaplet. He urges us to pray this Chaplet unceasingly, (Diary 810), drawing upon His passion (Diary 811) for mercy on us and on the whole world (Diary 475, 476).

The Chaplet of Divine Mercy is so special and urgent, because it is one of God's vessels to fulfill His plan to have mercy on all (Rom. 11:32).

The Three O'Clock Hour

The three o'clock hour is the time of the Lord Jesus' death on the Cross. It was the hour of grace for the whole world - mercy triumphed over justice (Diary 1572).

On Good Friday at 3:00 in 1935 (Diary 414) and again in 1936, Sister Faustina had a vision of the Lord Jesus crucified, who looked at her and said, "I thirst." Two rays issued from His side just as they appeared in the image. She felt a great desire to save souls and empty herself for the sake of poor sinners. She offered herself together with the dying

Jesus, to the Eternal Father, for the salvation of the whole world, with, in, and through Jesus (Diary 648).

A year later, at 3:00 o'clock on Good Friday of 1937, Sister Faustina was praying prostrate, in the form of a cross, interceding for the whole world at the moment of the death of Jesus. She heard the seven last words of Jesus. Then, He looked at her and said, "Beloved daughter of My Heart, you are My solace amidst terrible torments" (see Diary 1058).

These visions and words recall the Image of the merciful Savior, and the Chaplet of Divine Mercy as a preview of the vessel of the three o'clock hour devotion asked by our Lord in October of 1937 (Diary 1320) and February 1938 (Diary 1572). What Sister Faustina did at the visions of Christ crucified on Good Friday of 1935, 1936, and 1937, the Lord later asked of her to do every time the clock struck the three o'clock hour:

> If only for a brief moment, immerse yourself in My passion, particularly in My abandonment at the moment of agony. This is the hour of great mercy for the whole world. I will allow you to enter into My mortal sorrow. In this hour, I will refuse nothing to the soul that makes a request of me in virtue of My Passion (Diary 1320).

As Sister Faustina offered herself for sinners on Good Friday, Our Lord asks her to do the same each day:

> At 3:00 o'clock, implore My mercy, especially for sinners (Diary 1320).

Our Lord reminded Sister Faustina that at that hour she should immerse herself completely in His mercy, adoring and glorifying it, invoking its omnipotence for the whole world, and particularly for poor sinners; for at that moment mercy was opened wide for everyone (see Diary 1572).

Again, this word of Our Lord recalls the vision of Christ crucified (Diary 648).

In this hour you can obtain everything for yourself and for others for the asking; it is the hour of grace for the whole world (Diary 1572).

Our Lord asks Sister Faustina to respond to this hour with some suggested devotional practices: making the Stations of the Cross, if possible, or adoring the merciful Heart of Jesus in the Blessed Sacrament, or at least immersing herself in prayer if only for a brief instant (cf. Diary 1572).

The reason behind His special request for veneration of His passion at this hour is that our Lord wants all to venerate His mercy:

I claim veneration for My mercy from all creatures (Diary 1572).

and especially from Sister Faustina to whom He gave the most profound understanding of His mercy (Diary 1572).

Since God's plan is "to have mercy on all", (Rom. 11:32) He wants all to receive it by venerating and trusting His mercy. And in the three o'clock vessel, He has given us yet another special instrument to draw on His infinite mercy, another reminder of the urgency of His message of mercy. The three o'clock hour is the hour Peter and John went to the temple to pray (Acts 3:1). This Jewish hour of prayer is the traditional time of the evening sacrifice, giving the chaplet an added scriptural richness.

The Novena Before the Feast of Divine Mercy

The Lord asked Sister Faustina to prepare for the Feast of Divine Mercy with a novena of prayer. In 1936, the novena starting on Good Friday consisted of praying the Chaplet of Divine Mercy for nine days before the Feast of Mercy. "By this Novena, I will grant every possible grace to souls" (Diary 796), Our Lord promised. In 1937, Jesus again commanded her to make a novena before the Feast of Mercy, (Diary 1059), which she later wrote down (Diary 1209). She was to make this novena **for the conversion of the whole world and for**

the recognition of the Divine Mercy..." so that every soul will praise My Goodness. I desire trust from My creatures" (Diary 1059).

Our Lord instructed Sister Faustina to bring souls to the fount of His mercy, so that, they might draw strength and refreshment and whatever graces they need in the hardship of the human condition, especially at the hour of death. Each day she was to bring a different group of souls and immerse them in the ocean of His mercy. And the Lord Jesus promised that He would bring these souls into the house of His Father. He further promised that He would not deny anything to the souls she brought to the fount of His mercy, begging the Father for them on the strength of His bitter passion (see Diary 1209).

The Lord Jesus Himself gave Sister Faustina the different souls He wanted prayed for on each of the nine days: all mankind (especially sinners), priests, religious, devout and faithful souls, pagans and those who do not know Jesus, heretics and schismatics,, meek and humble souls and little children, those who especially venerate and glorify His mercy, those in purgatory, and lukewarm souls. All are to be immersed in the ocean of His mercy.

The fact of a novena, nine days of prayerful preparation and waiting, echoes the great novena in preparation for the outpouring of the Holy Spirit. The Acts of the Apostles tell us that the apostles, disciples, the women, and Mary, the Mother of Jesus, were in constant prayer (Acts 1:14) from the day of the ascension of our Lord Jesus into heaven, until the day of Pentecost. On that day, the Holy Spirit filled the place in which they were gathered and came upon them like tongues of fire (Acts 2:1-4). The Novena of Divine Mercy prepares with prayerful expectation for the great outpouring of God's merciful love on all who trust and glorify His mercy.

This vessel of the novena of Divine Mercy is yet another special instrument which to immerse all in His ocean of mercy, that all may glorify His mercy and prepare for His coming again.

Chapter 9

SISTER FAUSTINA:
THE SPECIAL DAUGHTER
OF MARY, THE MOTHER OF GOD

On the day of her perpetual vows, Sister Faustina addressed Mary and prayed:

> Mother of God, Most Holy Mary, my Mother, you are my mother in a **special way** because your beloved Son is my Bridegroom, and thus we are both your children. For your Son's sake, you have to love me. O Mary, my dearest Mother, guide my spiritual life in such a way that it will please your Son (Diary 240).

This prayer of Sister Faustina on the day of her spiritual nuptials to Jesus was answered by Mary in an extraordinary way when Mary appeared to her and said:

> My daughter, at God's command I am to be, in a special and exclusive way your Mother; but I desire that you, too, in a special way be my child (Diary 1414).

In a **special and exclusive way was** she to be daughter to Mary by the command of God! Mary, the Mother of God, was to be Mother of Sister Faustina preparing her for a special mission. On the feast of the Annunciation, March 25, 1936, the Mother of God appeared to Sister Faustina explaining her mission:

> I gave the Savior to the world; as for you, you have to **speak to the world about His great mercy and prepare the world for the Second Coming** of Him who will come, not as a merciful Savior, but as a just Judge. ... speak to souls about this great mercy while it is still time for mercy. If you keep silent now, you will be answering for a great number of souls on that terrible day. Fear nothing. Be faithful to the end. I sympathize with you (Diary 635).

"Speak to the world about His great mercy and prepare for His second coming." That is the mission of Sister Faustina and an awesome one it is! Mary's role was to prepare her special daughter by being a Mother to her, guiding and teaching her about the life of union with God, and strengthening her in sufferings by suffering along with her with sympathy and compassion. (Diary 25, 309, 316, 635).

On her part, Sister Faustina prayed to the Mother of God for this mission throughout her life. She began early in her vocation when she prayed to the Mother of God for guidance in finding a convent to enter: "Mary, lead me, guide me" (Diary 11). She consecrated herself to Mary, giving herself into her hands as Mother, asking for purity of heart, soul and body, and defense against all enemies" (Diary 79). She prayed, "Mary unite me with Jesus" (Diary 162). She regularly celebrated the feasts of Mary (e.g. Christmas, Presentation, Annunciation, Assumption) with special anticipation and joy even with novenas (Diary 1413). The rosary of our Lady was part of her prayer (Diary 412, 489, 515, 696, 709). In preparation for receiving Holy Communion, she earnestly asked the Mother of God to help her to prepare her soul for the coming of Mary's Son and to enkindle in her the fire of God's love, such as burned in Mary's heart at the time of the Incarnation of God (see Diary 1114). She prayed to be prepared.

Mary, on her part, asked for what was needed for Sister Faustina and her mission. She asked and obtained for her the great grace of purity (Diary 40), reflecting Mary's own Immaculateness. Further, Mary asked Sister Faustina to excercise her mission when sick by prayer.

> My daughter, what I demand of you is prayer, prayer, and once again prayer, for the world and especially for your country. For nine days receive Holy Communion in atonement and unite yourself closely to the Holy Sacrifice of the Mass. During these nine days you will stand before God as an offering; always and everywhere, at all times and places, day or night, whenever you wake up, pray in the spirit. In spirit, one can always remain in prayer (Diary 325).

Also, as a preparation for her mission Mary asked Sister to be faithful to the will of God, putting it ahead of sacrifices and holocausts (Diary 1244). As her special and dearly beloved daughter, Mary asked that she practice the three virtues most dear to her and most pleasing to God:

> The first is humility, humility, and once again humility; the second virtue, purity, the third virtue, love of God. Oh my daughter, you must especially radiate these virtues (Diary 1415).

With humility, purity, and love, she would be equipped for her mission of mercy.

In further preparation for the mission, Mary as a Mother instructed her in the interior life: to love God interiorly (Diary 40), to carry out His will in all things (Diary 40), to commune with God with intimacy (Diary 454), to accept all from God (Diary 529), to keep her eyes on the cross (Diary 561), to adore the Holy Trinity (Diary 564), and to live for God (Diary 620). The reception of Holy Communion was a special time for these instructions (Diary 840).

Sister Faustina reflected that "the more I imitate the Mother of God, the more deeply I get to know God" (Diary 843). For Sister, Mary was truly her mother (Diary 330), and she could nestle close to her Immaculate Heart like a little child (Diary 1097).

Sister Faustina was a special daughter of the Mother of God in order that she could be prepared by Mary for a special mission:

> Proclaiming God's Mercy in preparation for the Lord's coming again (cf. Diary 429, 635).

Chapter 10

THE SPECIAL TRAITS OF THE
SPIRITUAL LIFE OF
SISTER FAUSTINA

What made Sister Faustina so special in her spiritual life were the virtues and characteristics by which she imitated Jesus Christ, her bridegroom. She most clearly identified with Christ in the very way Jesus identified Himself with the Father: by love and mercy, in humble obedience to the will of God with complete trust in offering Himself as a victim for sinners on the cross.

"Humble obedience to the will of God", stands out as a very special characteristic of the life of Sister Faustina, as she offered herself as a victim of love for sinners (more on the suffering as victim in another chapter). In this "humble obedience to the will of God", she not only imitated and identified with Jesus (see Phil. 2:7-8), but also with Mary, the Mother of God. Mary expressed her humble obedience to the will of God in her "fiat", in her response to the message of the angel Gabriel. "Behold, I am the handmaid of the Lord. May it be done to me according to your word"

(Lk. 1:38). Mary continued this "yes" to the Lord even to the cross as she stood there in silent offering (Jn. 19:25) with her heart pierced (Lk. 2:35). In her "humble obedience to the will of God," Sister Faustina was instructed by both Jesus and Mary in order to be fully identified with them.

On February 4, 1935: Jesus in a very graphic way instructed Sister to "cancel her own will absolutely" (Diary 372) by marking a large "X" through the words "From today on, my will does not exist," written out on a full page of her diary. On the opposite page she was to write, "From today on, I do the will of God everywhere, always, and in everything" (Diary 372). Jesus told Sister, "Know that when you mortify your self-will, then mine reigns within you" (Diary 365).

On February 7, 1937, the Lord said, "I demand of you a perfect and whole-burnt offering; an offering of your will. No other sacrifice can compare with this one..." (Diary 923). In the rest of His instruction, He points out something that is significant in understanding His inability to begin the new congregation she was asked to found (Diary 435, 436, 615, 624) and the prohibition of the devotion to Divine Mercy (Diary 378, 1659):

> ... I know what you can do. I myself will give you many orders directly, but I will delay the possibility of their being carried out (Diary 923).

In her life, she strove to live out this instruction (Diary 830) seeking to make her own the words of Jesus: "I have come to do your will, O God" (Heb. 10:7); Not my will but yours be done (Lk. 22:42); Doing the will of Him who sent me and bringing His work to completion is my food" (Jn. 4:34). "I do always what pleases Him." (Jn. 8:29). Sister recorded that "I nourish myself on the will of God. It is my food" (Diary 886). "There is one word I need and continually ponder; it is everything to me; I live by it and die by it, and it is the holy will of God. It is my daily food. My whole soul listens intently to God's wishes. I do always what

God asks of me, although my nature often quakes and I feel that the magnitude of these things is beyond my strength. I know well what I am of myself, but I also know what the grace of God is, which supports me" (Diary 652).

How beautifully this reflects the Magnificat of Mary: "The mighty one has done great things for me" (Lk. 2:49) and the blessing Mary received from Jesus: "Blessed are those who hear the word of God and observe it" (Lk. 11:28).

Sister Faustina learned well the lesson of doing God's will:

> The Lord Jesus gave me to know how very pleasing to Him is a soul who lives in accordance with the will of God. It thereby gives very great glory to God (Diary 821, 724, 952).

Sister Faustina was also instructed in **humility** by her confessor Father Andrasz saying, "Humility, humility, ever humility, as we can do nothing of ourselves; all is purely and simply God's grace" (Diary 55); and humility be the characteristic traits of your soul... God's graces flow only into humble souls" (Diary 55). Our Lord made it plain to her that He demanded humility like His own (Diary 758) and that by her humility she pleased Him (Diary 532, 1092, 1222, 1563).

The Blessed Mother also instructed Sister in humility: "I desire, my dearly beloved daughter, that you practice the three virtues that are dearest to me—and most pleasing to God. The first is humility, humility, and once again humility..." (Diary 1415). Sister went to Mary to be penetrated by her humility (Diary 843) and asked Mary for her help to obtain deep humility (Diary 1306). Mary taught her to hear everything with humility (Diary 786).

Sister Faustina learned her lesson of humility very well and she grew in this humility by humiliations: "Humiliation is my daily food" (Diary 92); she was humiliated by her sisters and even by superiors (Diary 128, 129, 133). She recorded for us her understanding of humility in writing that nothing is better for the soul than humiliations; tribulations result in deep humility; only the humble are truly happy; a humble soul does not trust itself; it is defended by God (see Diary 115, 593), "There are so few saints because so few are deeply humble" (Diary 1306), she concludes, in her canticle of praise of humility.

Sister Faustina learned well the lesson of Jesus: "Take my yoke upon you and learn from me, for I am meek and humble of heart" (Mt. 11:29), (Diary 1220-1221). Toward the end of her life when Jesus again expressed His choice of her as His secretary of His mercy, she recorded her lesson of humility:

> At that moment I stirred myself in profound humility before God's majesty. But the more I humbled myself, the more God's presence penetrated me (Diary 1605).

with boldness she could say:

> Although you are great, Lord, you allow yourself to be overcome by a lowly and deeply humble soul. O humility, the most precious of virtues how few possess you! … Lord, reduce me to nothingness in my own eyes that I may find grace in yours (Diary 1436).

Sister Faustina was also instructed in **obedience** by Jesus:

> I have come to do my Father's will. I obeyed my parents, I obeyed my tormentors and now I obey the priests (Diary 535).

By her perpetual vow of obedience, she imitated Christ. She strived to live out her obedience to her religious superiors and spiritual director in everything as we see evidenced in her writings throughout her diary. For example:

I try always to be obedient despite everything (Diary 624).

When she didn't have the physical strength to carry out the duties of a porter, she learned that obedience infuses the soul and brings power to act (see Diary 1378, 1686). When asked by Our Lord to go to Mother Superior for permission to do penance by wearing a hair shirt and pray during the night for seven days, her superior said, "absolutely not!" When Sister then complained to the Lord He said; "I was here during your conversation with the superior and know everything. I don't demand mortification from you, but obedience. By obedience you give great glory to me" (Diary 28).

The Lord continued to train sister in obedience throughout her life, as can be seen in the various stages and struggles of trying to obey the Lord in establishing the new congregation of sisters (Diary 1263, 496, 981, see 536-537 for a general summary of the new congragation). In this suffering along with her increasing weakness from tuberculosis, she became more and more identified with Christ in His humble obedience to the will of God:

> ... He emptied Himself and took the form of a slave, being born in the likeness of men. He was known to be of human estate, and it was thus that He humbled Himself, obediently accepting even death, death on a cross! (Phil. 2:7-8).

In the midst of this push and pull of God's will, Sister Faustina again makes a total oblation of herself (Diary 1264).

The bottom line of this growing in "humble obedience to the will of God" is what Jesus said to her:

> With no other soul do I unite myself as closely and in such a way as I do with you, and this because of

the deep humility and ardent love you have for me (Diary 587).

Jesus told me that the most perfect and holy soul is the one that does the will of the Father...He told me that I was doing the will of God perfectly, and for this reason I am uniting myself with you and communing with you in a special and intimate way (Diary 603).

"In a special and intimate way" describes the special union of the Lord with Sister Faustina which equipped her for her special mission of mercy. Mary's humble obedience to the will of God equipped her to be the Mother of God in His first coming. The similar humble obedience to the will of God by Sister Faustina equipped her to proclaim God's mercy to prepare for His second coming.

Chapter 11

THE SPECIAL SUFFERING OF SISTER FAUSTINA

Through her sufferings, Sister Faustina lived fully the words of St. Paul:

> I have been crucified with Christ, and the life I live now is not my own (Gal. 2:19-20).

In her mission of mercy, Sister was called by Our Lord Jesus to be completely identified with Him in His passion. The passion of Christ was the moment of His greatest identification with our human condition and the moment of the bursting of His flood of mercy on the whole world. Identification with this boundless source of mercy was the essence of her mission.

Sister Faustina suffered the passion of Christ, because Jesus **asked** her to make an offering of herself for sinners:

> I desire that you make an offering of yourself for sinners and especially for souls who have lost hope in God's mercy (Diary 308).

I desire that you be entirely transformed into love and that you burn ardently as a pure victim of love (Diary 726).

Our Lord made it known to her that this identification with Him on the Cross was the way to save souls:

I want your last moments to be completely similar to mine on the cross. There is but one price at which souls are bought and that is suffering united to my suffering on the cross (Diary 324).

Our Lord makes it clear to Sister that she was participating in the great work of Salvation:

I am giving you a share in the redemption of mankind (Diary 310).

Help me, my daughter, to save souls. Join your sufferings to my passion and offer them to the heavenly Father for sinners (Diary 1032).

I have need of your sufferings to rescue souls (Diary 1612).

This participation in the passion of Christ conformed Sister to Himself:

When your mind is dimmed and your suffering is great, it is then that you take an active part in my passion, and I am comforming you more fully to myself (Diary 1697).

It was like a school where Jesus taught her to suffer (see Diary 1626), giving her an "exclusive privilege" to drink from the cup which He drank (Diary 1626).

This "exclusive privilege" to suffer with Christ and like Christ was offered to Sister, but she had to make a **free-will consent** to it. The Lord would not force her. He would not lessen His graces and would still continue His intimate relationship with her even if she did not consent to make this sacrifice (Diary 135). The whole mystery of participating in Christ's suffering, echoing St. Paul's share in the sufferings of Christ (see Col 1:24), depended on the free consent to the sacrifice, given freely with full use of her faculties. The whole power and value of this sacrifice lies in this free and conscious act (Diary 136). Sister responded in words that echoed the response of the Blessed Virgin Mary to the message of the angel Gabriel:

> Do with me as you please. I subject myself to your will... (Diary 136).

She realized that she was entering into an extraordinary communion with the incomprehensable majesty of God. A great mystery took place! She thought she would die of love at the sight of His glance (see Diary 136-138). And the Lord said to her:

> You are the delight of my Heart; from today on, every one of your acts, even the smallest, will be a delight to my eyes, whatever you do (Diary 137).

and Sister recorded:

> At that moment I felt transconsecrated. My earthly body was the same but my soul was different; God was now living in it with the totality of His delight. This was not a feeling, but a conscious reality that nothing can obscure (Diary 137).

Sister was equipped to begin her mission of mercy in this identification with Christ and she experienced it immediately: "suffering seemed to spring out of the ground" (Diary 138).

Later sister wrote out a full act of oblation of accepting totally God's will and all sufferings, in union with Christ's suffering - all for sinners (Diary 309). She renewed this oblation daily by the prayer:

> O Blood and Water which gushed forth from the Heart of Jesus as a fount of mercy for us I trust in you (Diary 309).

She later recorded another prayer of oblation (Diary 1264), and then, toward the end of her life she offered her death as a holocaust for sinners (Diary 1680).

In this mission mercy, and Sister Faustina suffered terribly, not only from her fellow sisters and from her tuberculosis, but especially by experiencing the very passion of Christ in her own body. She received the "exclusive privilege" to share in the pain of His passion as the way of exercising her mission of rescuing souls.

Some three dozen times sister records her experience of the passion in an invisible manner (Diary 964, 976), and it was "all for souls" (e.g. Diary 759, 931, 1010, 1468, 1627). She would experience pain in her hands and feet when in the presence of someone in sin (Diary 705, 1079, 1196, 1274, 1305, 1536). Our Lord taught her to see His love and mercy for sinners in His passion:

> Look into my Heart and see there the love and mercy which I have for mankind, and especially sinners. Look and enter into my passion (Diary 1663).

She recorded her response:

> In an instant, I experienced and lived through the whole passion of Jesus in my own heart. I was sur-

prised that these tortures did not deprive me of my life (Diary 1663).

The Lord Jesus taught Sister Faustina very well that "the bride must resemble her Betrothed" (Diary 268). After all, she was a disciple of a crucified Master (Diary 1513).

Throughout her diary, Sister Faustina described the precious and special place suffering had in her life. She learned her lesson well: "Suffering is a great grace, by it we become like Jesus Our Savior (Diary 38,57); God is nearest to a soul that suffers (Diary 109); My name is sacrifice (Diary 135); daily food; the moment I came to love suffering, it ceased to be suffering for me (Diary 276); Suffering is a delight, only love lends value to it (Diary 303, 351); Suffering is a thermometer which measures the love of God in the soul (Diary 774); I long for the salvation of souls... In sacrifice my heart will find free expression (Diary 235); Sacrifice alone is nothing, but joined with Christ it is all-powerful (Diary 482); I'm nicknamed 'the dump' of other's pain (Diary 871); Chosen souls uphold the world in existence (Diary 926); If only suffering souls knew how loved they are by God! - someday we'll know the value of suffering but we will no longer be able to suffer (Diary 963); The quintessence of love is sacrifice and suffering (Diary 1103); Souls become useful by sacrifice as God's love flows through it, because everything is concentrated in this love and takes its value from it" (Diary 1358).

Six months before she died, Sister Faustina reflected on her life of suffering and the mystery of God's ways:

O Christ, if my soul had known all at once, what it was going to have to suffer during her lifetime, it would have died of terror at the sight; it would not have touched its lips to the cup of bitterness. But as it has been given to me drink it has a drop at a time, it has emptied the cup to the very bottom... (Diary 1655; see also 694, 697).

I do not know how to describe all that I suffer and what I have written thus far is merely a drop. There are moments of suffering about which I really cannot write. ... There are times when the Lord Himself allows terrible sufferings, and then again there are times when He does not let me suffer and removes everything that might afflict my soul. These are His ways, unfathomable and incomprehensible to us. It is for us to submit ourselves completely to His holy will. There are many mysteries never fathomed here on earth; eternity will reveal them (Diary 1656).

The sufferings of Sister Faustina identified her completely with the crucified Savior (cf. Gal 2:19-20) and made her a special vessel of His mercy in this life and the next (Diary 281, 1209).

Chapter 12

THE SPECIAL PLACE OF THE
HOLY EUCHARIST IN THE LIFE
OF SISTER FAUSTINA

Sister Maria Faustina of the Blessed Sacrament is her full name and the key to her life was the Holy Eucharist. Almost every page of her diary makes a reference to the Eucharist. She makes this revealing statement about her life:

> The most solemn moment of my life is the moment when I receive Holy Communion and for every Holy Communion I give thanks to the Most Holy Trinity (Diary 1804).

How Sister rejoiced when her secret desire was fulfilled again and again as she drew by lot her New Year's Patron: "The Most Blessed Eucharist" (Diary 360).

There are a number of "special" aspects of her relationship to the Holy Eucharist, among them is her profound **understanding** of the mystery of this gift of God. She describes it as the **greatest** gift of His presence:

During Mass, I thanked the Lord Jesus for having deigned to redeem us and for having given us the **greatest of all gifts;** (Diary 1670).

You wanted to stay with us, and so you left us yourself in the Sacrament of the Altar, and you opened wide your mercy to us. ... You opened an inexhaustible spring of mercy for us, giving your dearest possion, the Blood and Water, from Your Heart (Diary 1747).

During a Holy Hour, in a vision of the cenacle, Sister saw the institution of the Holy Eucharist. She came to understand that, "At the moment of consecration... the sacrifice was fully consummated. Now, only the external ceremony of death will be carried out - external destruction; **the essence is in the Cenacle**. Never in my whole life had **I understood this mystery so profoundly** as during that hour of adoration" (Diary 684, 757, 832).

She then goes on to pray that all may come to know the mystery of the Eucharist.

Oh, how ardently I desire that the whole world would come to know this unfathomable mercy (Diary 684).

She came to know His majesty in the Cenacle and at the same time:

His great humbling of Himself (Diary 757).

Sister expresses the depth of the mystery as a mystery of mercy:

Who will ever conceive and understand the depth of mercy that gushed forth from your Heart? (Diary 832).

It is only in eternity that we shall know the great mystery effected in us by Holy Communion. O most precious moments of my life (Diary 840).

O what awesome mysteries take place during Mass!
... One day we will know what God is doing for us
in each Mass, and what sort of gift He is preparing
in it for us (Diary 914).

... the miracle of Your mercy. All the tongues of men
and angels united could not find words adequate to
this mystery of Your love and mercy (Diary 1489).

A very special aspect of Sister's life was her desire to be
transformed into a **living Host**, a wafer, hidden and broken
to be given to others:

Jesus, transform me, miserable and sinful as I am,
into Your own self (for you can do all things), and
give me to Your Eternal Father. I want to be a **sacrifi-
cial host** before you, but an ordinary wafer to people.
I want the fragrance of my sacrifice to be known to
You alone (Diary 483 see also Diary 641, 832, 1289,
1392, 1622, 1564, 1826).

Transform me in Yourself, O Jesus, that I may be a
living sacrifice and pleasing to You. I **desire to atone
at each moment for poor sinners** (Diary 908).

Jesus answered her prayers telling her:

You are a living host, pleasing to the Heavenly Father
(Diary 1826).

Sister Faustina felt this transformation as a holy fire present in her always:

All the good that is in me is due to Holy Communion. I owe everything to it. I feel this holy fire has
transformed me completely. Oh, how happy I am to
be a dwelling for You, O Lord! My heart is a temple
in which You dwell continually (Diary 1392).

Sister Faustina lived fully the prayer of the Church:

Come Holy Spirit, fill the hearts of the faithful and enkindle the fire of your divine love.

The experience of being a **living host**, hidden, broken, and given was the central experience of her life - But, this experience was based on the **union** of love with the living God. And this union was most profoundly experienced in conjunction with the Holy Eucharist, either during Mass and Holy Communion, or during adoration of the Blessed Sacrament. Her union with the Lord was, in His words, as a bride:

Here, I am entirely yours, soul, body and divinity as Your Bridegroom. You know what love demands, one thing only, reciprocity (Diary 1770).

As a bride, she prepared for Holy Communion saying:

I am preparing myself for Your coming as a bride does for the coming of her bridegroom (Diary 1805).

At times she experienced during Holy Communion a union with the Holy Trinity:

At that moment, I was drawn into the bosom of the Most Holy Trinity, and I was immersed in the love of the Father, the Son and the Holy Spirit. These moments are hard to describe (Diary 1670) (See also Diary 1121, 1129).

These times of union are a "mystery of love" in the words of the Lord Jesus (Diary 156) and a taste of eternity (Diary 969).

Holy Communion was the **strength and support** of Sister Faustina in her day's struggle (Diary 91). The Lord taught her: "In the Host is your power; it will defend you" (Diary 616). She said that the Eucharist was her strength from her tender years:

Once, when I was seven years old at a Vespers Service, conducted before the Lord Jesus in the monstrance, the love of God was imparted to me for the first time and filled my little heart; and the Lord gave me understanding of divine things (Diary 1404).

Throughout her diary, she recorded the strength she received from the Eucharist (see Diary 91, 616, 814, 876, 1404, 1489, 1509, 1620).

A special gift given to Sister Faustina was the **continuous presence** of the Eucharist from one Holy Communion until the next. During midnight Mass, 1935, after Holy Communion she heard:

> I am always in your heart; not only when you receive me in Holy Communion, but always (Diary 575).

> I have come to know that Holy Communion remains in me until the next Holy Communion (Diary 1302).

Throughout the day she adored Jesus, praising and asking Him for graces, especially for children (Diary 1821).

A regular experience for Sister was the **vision** of the Lord during Holy Mass. Over sixty such visions are recorded in her diary, mostly of the infant Jesus, a few occasions with the Blessed Mother, and at other times, Jesus during His passion and some of His majesty. Some dozen times she records seeing the rays of mercy as in the image of the Merciful Savior coming from the Holy Eucharist, at times covering the world (See Diary 420, 441, 1046).

The Holy Eucharist was a precious **time of teaching** for Sister Faustina by Our Lord Jesus about: her mission of winning souls (Diary 1690), the way to live a spiritual life by abiding in Him (Diary 1685), His desire to give graces in the Eucharist (Diary 1705), praying in union with Mary (Diary 32), offering to the Father the Blood and Wounds of Jesus in the Mass as an act of expiation for sins, and the great mystery of the institution of the Holy Eucharist (Diary 684, 757, 832). The Lord used the time of Holy Communion as a time of profound teaching.

These profound experiences and teachings during the Holy Eucharist were closely associated with the **vessels of mercy:** The feast, the image, the chaplet, and the three o'clock remembrance. Reception of Holy Communion is integral to the celebration of the Feast of Divine Mercy. As said above, on a number of occasions, Sister saw the Eucharist radiate with rays like in the Image of the Merciful Savior. The chaplet of Divine Mercy is Eucharistic. It is an offering of the Body and Blood, Soul and Divinity of the Lord Jesus Christ, to the Father, in atonement for the sins of the world. One of the the devotions suggested by Our Lord to honor the hour of His death is to adore, in the Blessed Sacrament, His heart, which is full of Mercy (Diary 1572). The vessels the Lord gave us through Sister Faustina are Eucharistic.

The special place of the Holy Eucharist in the life of Sister Faustina can be summed up in her full official name, Sister Maria Faustina of the Blessed Sacrament and in the name she called herself. After her oblation, "My name is to be 'sacrifice' " (Diary 135). The Lord Jesus summed up her life in what He called her: "You are a living host" (Diary 1826).

Her greatest desire was to be Eucharist, hidden, like Jesus, blessed by her union with the Lord, broken like Jesus in the passion and totally given for the salvation of souls. Her prayer to be consecrated sums up her life:

I am a white host before You, O Divine Priest. Consecrate me Yourself, and may my transubstantiation be known only to You. I stand before You each day as a sacrificed host and implore Your mercy upon the world (Diary 1564).

Chapter 13

SISTER FAUSTINA'S MISSION OF MERCY IS THE SPECIAL OBJECT OF SATAN'S HATE

The mission of Sister Faustina in proclaiming mercy by her writing and winning souls by her suffering and prayer was so effective that Satan and his demons were furious with rage and jealousy. She was the special object of their hatred for making known God's mercy and saving souls, but our Lord protected her:

> You are united to me; fear nothing. But know, my child, that Satan hates you; he hates every soul, but he burns with a particular hatred for you, because you snatched so many souls from his dominion (Diary 412).

Satan would distract her during her writing, grinding his teeth (Diary 1583), tempting her not to write of God's goodness (Diary 96-97), telling her not to think of this work of mercy, because God is not as merciful as she says (Diary 1405). Satan would tempt her to discouragement, making speeches about the fidelity of her work and telling her, "Never to speak of God's mercy. Why bother about other souls" (Diary 1497-1499). He admitted his hatred for Sister Faustina and the mercy of God (Diary 1167). He asked her, like his temptation of Jesus (Lk. 4:7), that she glorify him (Diary 520).

The response of Sister Faustina to these temptations of Satan was to "Glorify the Lord alone" (Diary 520). She continued to write and to pray and suffer for souls. She was so effective in her mission of mercy that the demons cried out that "you are beginning to torment us even in hell" (Diary 323).

Our Lord taught Sister Faustina how to battle violently. After a prolonged temptation from Satan (Diary 1496 to 1498) the Lord Jesus encouraged her:

> I am pleased with what you are doing. And you can continue to be at peace if you always do the best you can in respect to this work of mercy. **Be absolutely as frank as possible with your confessor.** Satan gained nothing by tempting you, because you did not enter into conversation with him. Continue to act in this way. **You gave Me great glory** today by fighting so faithfully. Let it be confirmed and engraved on your heart that I am always with you, even if you don't feel My presence at the time of battle (Diary 1499).

"You give Me great glory!" The glory of God is the issue in making known His mercy. Satan does not want God glorified by souls turning to Him and receiving His mercy.

"Be absolutely as frank as possible with your confessor!" This is the Lord's instruction for Sister Faustina's protection. She was given a confessor and spiritual director to guide her and make clear to her the word of the Lord (Diary 639, 967, 968).

During a conference on spiritual warfare Our Lord told sister to have trust and recourse not only to Himself but also to her spiritual director and confessor (Diary 1760).

Sister Faustina was very faithful and open with her spiritual director Father Michael Sopocko. She saw him as a priest whom God loved greatly (Diary 676), but whom Satan hates terribly, because he is leading many souls to a high degree of sanctity and has **regard only for God's glory** (Diary 1384).

Again, God's glory is at issue in the work of Divine Mercy. Sister saw this glory and shared her vision of the victory of Divine Mercy a few months before she died:

> I saw the glory of God which flows from the image. Many souls are receiving graces, although they do not speak of it openly. Even though it has met up with all sorts of vicissitudes, **God is receiving glory** because of it; and the efforts of Satan and of evil men are shattered and come to naught. In spite of Satan's anger, The **Divine Mercy will triumph over the whole world and will be worshipped by all souls** (Diary 1789; see also 378, 1659).

The Divine Mercy - the God of Mercy - will triumph over the whole world and all will glorify Him. This is the fulfillment of the plan of God recorded for us in St. Paul's letter to the Romans:

> That God may have mercy on all! (Rom 11:32)

Satan by the very fact of his anger at God's mercy, thereby acknowledges the glory of God's mercy. In our battle of life, the great weapon of victory given to us is to glorify God's infinite mercy that saves all who turn to Him.

Glory be to your infinite merciful love!

Chapter 14

THE SPECIAL AFFINITY OF
THE DIARY OF SISTER FAUSTINA
AND THE ENCYCLICAL OF
JOHN PAUL II, RICH IN MERCY

A comprehensive study in order to indicate the **affinity of ideas** found in the Diary of Sister Faustina and the encyclical "Rich in Mercy" (not to mention their probable interdependence) would be most welcome. These salient points are numerous, for they draw their inspiration from the same source; namely, from revelation of God and the teaching of Christ.

This challenge was given by the then Archbishop Andrew M. Deskur, now cardinal, in his preface to the Polish edition of the "Diary of Sister Faustina", 1981, written soon after the publication "Rich in Mercy", November 30, 1980.

The salient points of affinity are certainly numerous, not in the exact words but in the ideas and themes developed in "Rich in Mercy." Certainly this is due to the common source of truth in Sacred Scripture and Church tradition about God's mercy. There is, however, a "probable inter-dependence" because of the personal role of the Holy Father as bishop and later as Cardinal Archbishop of Cracow. Some of the interdependence probably arises from his regular visits to the tomb of Sister Faustina as bishop, his active role initiating her cause for beautification, and his conscripting the leading theologian of Poland, Father Ignacy Rozycki, to review the Diary of Sister Faustina. In the explanation of the "Notification" of April 15, 1978 the Holy See credits Karol Cardinal Wotyla in lifting the ban on devotion to the mercy of God according to Sister Faustina:

> ... with the new 'Notification,'... arrived at in the light of original documentation examined also by the careful informative intervention of the then Archbishop of Cracow, Karol Cardinal Wojtyla, it was the intention of the Holy See to revoke the prohibition contained in the preceding 'Notification' of 1959... (July 12, 1979).

"The careful informative intervention" of Cardinal Wojtyla is a strong basis for "Interdependence" of the "Diary" and the Second Encyclical of the Holy Father, "Rich in Mercy". It is an interdependence, but not strictly based on the "Diary" which is not referred to in the encyclical. In no way could John Paul II refer to the "Diary" of Sister Faustina, because she is not yet beatified. His mentioning Sister Faustina would prejudice her cause and disrupt the normal procedure of the Congregation for the Causes of Saints.

The special affinity of ideas in the encyclical "Rich in Mercy" and the "Diary of Sister Faustina" can be shown in the **Schematic Summary** "Rich in Mercy" which gathers the key points in sweeping statements that can be used to teach, preach, and help to remember this message of mercy (G.W. Kosicki, 1987). The nine statements from the Schematic Summary are underlined and then followed by statements from the Diary that illustrate the affinity.

The Papal letter "Rich in Mercy" proclaims mercy as:

1. **THE prophetic word of our time: the now Word is Mercy!** "While there is still time, let them [all mankind] have recourse to the fount of My mercy; let them profit from the Blood and Water which gushed forth for them" (Diary 848, see also 83, 1159, 1160), our Lord told Sister.

2. **THE content, power and mission of Christ and His Church.** Sister Faustina's mission was to proclaim God's mercy to all [see Diary 50, 300, 301, 378, 379, 570, 687, 699, 848, 1074, 1142, 1190, 1396, 1448, 1516, 1666, 1728], by writing, by prayer and by her suffering. (see the chapter on "Why is Sister Faustina so Special?")

3. **THE summary of the Gospel: "Blessed are the merciful for they shall obtain mercy.** This text of Matthew 5:7 discribes the great circle of mercy (see chapter on "How do we enter the Circle of Mercy?). Sister Faustina records the words of Our Lord on how to be merciful: by trust in the Lord, by words and deeds, (Diary 742) she also lived out this gospel beatitude to perfection.

4. **THE parable of mercy: the prodigal son the essence of mercy in the restored value of man.** "My daughter," the Lord instructed her, "write about My mercy toward tormented souls... write that I am more generous toward sinners than toward the just. It was for their sake that I came down from heaven; it was for their sake that My Blood was spilled. Let them not fear to approach Me; they are most in need of My mercy" (Diary 1275, see also 1182, 1507, 1578, 1588).

5. **THE answer to the question of "a lack of peace."** "Mankind will have no peace until it turns with trust to My mercy" (Diary 300). For the Lord's description of "lack of peace" ("uneasiness" in –11 of "Rich in Mercy") recall the chapter "Mercy, Mercy, Mercy" God's mercy poured out on us and on the whole world is the only answer to the human condition.

6. **THE summons to the Church and by the Church to practice, preach, and plead for mercy** (cf. -2 and 15). The whole "Diary" is a summons to Sister Faustina and to us to proclaim mercy - in practice of deeds, words and prayer (e.g. Diary 742). Our Lord explained to her: "You are to show mercy to your neighbor always and everywhere. You must not shrink from this or try to excuse yourself from it" (Diary 742).

7. **THE revelation of Jesus, mercy incarnate, centered in the crucified, risen Jesus, continues in the Heart of Mary.** The sufferings of Sister Faustina identified her completely with the crucified Savior and made her a special vessel of His mercy (see the chapter on "The Special Sufferings of Sister Faustina"). The crucified Christ is the source of mercy: "O Blood and Water, which gushed forth from the Heart of Jesus as a fount of Mercy for us, I trust in You" (Diary 187). "On the cross, the fountain of My mercy was opened wide by a lance for all souls—no one have I excluded" (Diary 1182). Mary had a special relationship to Sister Faustina: "I am not only the Queen of Heaven, but also the Mother of Mercy and your Mother..." (Diary 330). (See the chapter "Sister Faustina the Special Daughter of Mary".)

8. **THE prayer for the presence of love which is greater than evil, sin, and death.** Sister Faustina was commissioned by the Lord to pray for mercy, appealing to His mercy, even pleading, especially for sinners (Diary 186), (see chapter on "Why is Sister Faustina so Special?") "My daughter, give Me souls. Know that it is your mission to win souls for Me by your prayer and sacrifice, and by encouraging them to trust in My mercy" (Diary 1690). Sister had a great gift of praying for the dying, for "love that is greater than death" (e.g. Diary 1698).

9. **THE plea for us and the whole world.** Our Lord told Sister Faustina: "Your assignment and duty here on earth is to **beg for mercy for the whole world**" (Diary 570). "Unceasingly say the chaplet that I have taught you" (Diary

687). This plea for mercy is the central message of the encyclical "Rich in Mercy" and the central prayer which our Lord asked of Sister:

> Eternal Father, I offer you the Body and Blood, soul and Divinity of Your dearly Beloved Son, Our Lord, Jesus Christ, in atonement for our sins and through the whole world. For the sake of His sorrowful Passion, **have mercy on us and on the whole world** (Diary 476).

This plea for mercy on the whole world is the summary of the encyclical "Rich in Mercy" and of the "Diary of Sister Faustina":

> Lord, have mercy on us and on the whole world!

The very subject matter of the encyclical on Divine Mercy gives a special affinity to the whole of the message and mission of the "Diary of Sister Faustina." This affinity is most important to help grasp why the Holy Father would choose to write on such a topic.

The bottom line of both the encyclical "Rich and Mercy" and the "Diary of Sister Faustina" is a clear message, put in three statements:

1. God is mercy itself.

2. His mercy is the only answer to our human condition.

3. Now is the time to turn to His mercy—repenting, trusting, pleading.

John Paul II wrote as a philosopher, theologian, poet, mystic and Pope. Sister Faustina, a simple nun and mystic, wrote with only three winters of schooling whatever the Lord Jesus taught her. Both give the same message, "The truth and challenge of the gospel" (John Paul II, Fatima, 1982):

Now is the time to turn to God's Mercy.

Chapter 15

THE SPECIAL DEVOTION OF SISTER FAUSTINA TO THE MERCIFUL HEART OF JESUS

Sister Faustina had a special devotion to the Merciful Heart of Jesus which expressed itself in living the message of Divine Mercy. Further, it was the message of the feast, the image, the chaplet, the three o'clock hour, the novena;
    lived with trust and mercy,
    all gathered into one,
    all to give glory to God.
She came to understand and experience that the Merciful Heart of Jesus is THE vessel of mercy.

In her devotion to the Merciful Heart of Jesus, Sister fulfilled to perfection the invitation of Jesus:
        Come to me, all you who labor
            and are burdened and
            I will give you rest.
        Take my yoke upon you and
        Learn from me for I am meek and humble of heart;
            and you will find rest

for yourselves. For my yoke
is easy and my burden light (Mt 11:28-30).

She did come to the Merciful Heart of Jesus in a profound union of hearts, finding the rest of peace; she took His cross as a victim of love for the sake of others; she learned mercy and humility from Jesus who formed her after the model of His own Heart.

She was able to learn so well, because Jesus Himself was her Teacher:

I was your teacher; I am and I will be; strive to make your heart like unto My humble and gentle Heart (Diary 1701).

Sister wrote of her Teacher:

He Himself forms my heart according to His divine wishes and likings, but always with much goodness and mercy. Our hearts are fused as one (Diary 1024).

Jesus reminded her of His yoke:

You often call Me your Master. This is pleasing to My Heart; but do not forget, My disciple, that you are a disciple of a crucified Master. Let that one word be enough for you. You know what is contained in the cross (Diary 1513).

Early on in her diary, Sister Faustina records the call of the Lord to **model her heart** on His Merciful Heart:

My daughter, I desire that your heart be formed after the model of My Merciful Heart. You must be completely imbued with My mercy (Diary 167, November 1932).

She prayed for this change of heart:

My Jesus, make My heart like unto Your Merciful

Heart Jesus, help me to go through life doing good to everyone (Diary 692, September 1936).

Near the end of her life (June 1938), she records the words of Our Lord in a **conference on mercy** in which He describes the results of His forming her heart on the model of His own Merciful Heart:

> My daughter, I desire that your heart be an abiding place of My mercy. I desire that this mercy flow out upon the whole world through your heart (Diary 1777).

God's desire and choice to use the heart of Sister Faustina was made possible by the **union of their hearts**. The Lord described her heart:

> My daughter, your heart is My heaven (Diary 238).

During the Mass of the day of her perpetual vows she prayed:

> I place my heart on the paten where Your Heart has been placed... Jesus, from now on Your Heart is mine, and mine is Yours alone (Diary 239).

And Jesus spoke to her:

> My spouse, **our hearts are joined forever.** Remember to Whom you have vowed (Diary 239 and 1754).

Throughout her diary Sister records **the Lord's words** about this **union of hearts**. Repeatedly Jesus reminds her that: He dwells in her heart always (Diary 78, 160, 575, 609, 723, 1011, 1133, 1140, 1181, 1346, 1499, 1722, 1777, 1820); She is the delight of His Heart (Diary 826, 980, 1061, 1078, 1176, 1193, 1513, 1824); He rested in her heart (Diary 268, 339, 866) and she was invited to rest on His heart (Diary 873, 902, 945, 1053, 1685); He called her close to His Merciful Heart (Diary

229, 730, 797, 1074, 1327, 1481, 1490, 1617); He found solace and comfort of Heart with her heart (Diary 164, 445, 580, 581, 1056, 1058); His Heart watches over her (Diary 799, 1542, 1700); His Heart answers her requests (Diary 294, 570, 718, 1489, 1722).

In a word echoing the word of the Father at Tabor (see Mt. 17:5), Jesus says: "My favor rests in your heart" (Diary 1774).

In a similar way **Sister Faustina** speaks of this **union of hearts** from her experience. In the early part of her diary she writes: "My heart is a permanent dwelling place for Jesus. No one but Jesus has access to it" (Diary 193, early, 1933). Near the end of her life in response to the Lord's question, "Do you not have any desires in your heart?" she answered:

"I have one great desire, and it is to be united with You forever" (Diary 1700, May 1938). Her heart experienced being pierced by a flame of love and completely transformed into Him (Diary 1140, see also 841, 943, 1050). She describes her heart dissolving in an ecstasy of love (Diary 1030, 1050, 1057, 1506, 1553, 1600), and her heart longing for the Lord (Diary 841, 867, 876, 886, 1026). She rests on the Heart of Jesus (Diary 801, 928, 1348), pressed by the Lord (Diary 869, 873, 1011) sensing His presence (Diary 582, 761, 903, 946, 1345, 1391, 1479, 1821), close to His Heart (Diary 733, 869, 1330, 1363), and rests unceasingly with Him in the depths of her heart (Diary 903).

Union of the heart of Sister Faustina with the Merciful Heart of Jesus is the foundation of her mission of mercy. By and through this union of hearts she is the apostle of His mercy as the Lord announced on the feast of the Most Sacred Heart (June 4, 1937). Sister records:

Today is the Feast of the Most Sacred Heart of Jesus. During Holy Mass, I was given the **knowledge of the Heart of Jesus** and of the nature of the fire of love with which He burns for us and of how His heart is an ocean of mercy. Then I heard a voice: **'Apostle of My Mercy**, proclaim to the whole world My unfathomable mercy' (Diary 1142).

Sister then continues to record the words of Our Lord describing her mission as an apostle and secretary of His mercy:

Do not be discouraged by the difficulties you encounter in proclaiming My mercy. These difficulties that affect you so painfully are needed for your sanctification (read **union of heart**) and as evidence that this work is Mine. My daughter, be diligent in writing down every sentence I tell you concerning My mercy, because this is meant for a great number of souls who will profit from it (Diary 1142).

Because of this union of hearts, Sister Faustina had a profound knowledge of the merciful Heart of Jesus and could write freely about it.

The Message of the Merciful Heart of Jesus

The Merciful Heart of Jesus gathers into one the various elements of the message of Divine Mercy described in the Diary of Sister Faustina. The Merciful Heart of Jesus focuses both the message and the devotion to His Divine Mercy on the person of Jesus, because it is the "divine-human Heart of Jesus" (See Diary 528) that is considered.

The Merciful Heart of Jesus can be considered as **the** vessel of mercy because it is the way our Lord Himself described it in His **Conference on Mercy** given to Sister Faustina:

My daughter, **know that My Heart is mercy itself.**

Then he goes on to describe the nature of His mercy flowing out on all:

From this **sea of mercy** graces flow out upon the whole world.

He continues with a description of the effect of His mercy on souls:

No soul that has approached Me has ever gone away unconsoled. All misery gets buried in the depths of My mercy.

Then He makes a sweeping statement:

Every saving and sanctifying grace flows from this foundation (Dairy 1777).

He then makes the statement of His desire that her heart be the abiding place of His mercy and that it flow out through her heart to the whole world (Diary 1777 as quoted above).

In the chapter **How does God describe His own mercy?**, we saw the way God speaks of His mercy. Here it is important to point out the way He speaks of His **Heart**. It is mercy itself (Diary 1777); it is the fountain of mercy (Diary 1190, 1520, see also 187, 309, 367, 1148, 1182, 1309, 1507, 1747); it is full of mercy (Diary 1190, 1447, 1572); it overflows (Diary 1148, 1183, 1309, 1507, 1777, 1689) especially for sinners (Diary 367, 1541); it becomes like a flame for souls (Diary 186, 304, 906, 1142, 1521), it never rejects the contrite (Diary 1485, 1488, 1682, 1728, 1729), it is a Heart that was pierced (Diary 299, 1182, 1485, 1520); it desires to be loved by all (Diary 1703); it gives comfort (Diary 1487, 1521). But it is also a Heart that is sensitive, pained, and wounded by the distrust, indifference, and ingratitude of souls (Diary 362, 367, 379, 580, 1288, 1385, 1478, 1486, 1532, 1537, 1577, 1598, 1658, 1683, 1702, 1717). It is saddening to note that most of these painful complaints of the Merciful Heart of Jesus are about religious and priests, His committed souls.

How beautifully Jesus describes His Heart as Mercy: "My Heart rejoices in this title of Mercy" (Diary 299).

The Merciful Heart of Jesus, which is the very person of Jesus, is the **unifying element** of the message and devotion to the Divine Mercy. This can be seen in the close parallel of the first vision of the Merciful Heart of Jesus (Diary 177) and the first vision of the Lord Jesus as depicted in the image (see Diary 47 to 50 and the explanation 299).

> After the renewal of vows (in the year 1932) and Holy Communion, I suddenly saw the Lord Jesus, who said to me with great kindness, **"My daughter, look at My Merciful Heart."** As I fixed my gaze on the Most Sacred Heart, the same rays of light, as are represented in the image as blood and water, came from it, and I understood how great is the Lord's mercy. And again Jesus said to me with kindness, "My daughter, speak to priests about this inconceivable mercy of Mine. The flames of mercy are burning Me - clamoring to be spent; I want to keep pouring them out upon souls; souls just don't want to believe My goodness (Diary 177).

In both visions, the Lord Jesus appears with rays of light representing His blood and water coming from His Heart. Sister gazes upon the Lord and then is told to address priests about His mercy which is like flames burning Him, clamoring to be spent, which He wants to pour out upon souls, but there is so much distrust.

In the vision of the Lord to be painted, Sister is told to follow the pattern she sees and add the signature, "Jesus I trust in you." Our Lord then promises eternal life, protection, and victory here on earth to those venerate this image (Diary 47-48). The image is to be blessed on the feast of Divine Mercy (Diary 49).

Even these aspects of the first vision are echoed in terms of the Merciful Heart of Jesus. Sister Faustina's heart is to be formed according to the pattern she sees in the Merciful Heart of Jesus. He is the model (Diary 167), teacher (Diary 1701), and master (Diary 1513), as described above. She is also taught a prayer of trust:

> O Blood and Water which gushed forth from the Heart Jesus as a fount of Mercy for us, I trust in You (Diary 186-187).

Our Lord also makes a promise regarding his Merciful Heart which summarizes much of the message of mercy:

> Tell aching mankind to snuggle close to My Merciful Heart, and I will fill it with peace (Diary 1074).

The Merciful Heart of Jesus as a unifying element of the devotion to the Divine Mercy has a fascinating relationship to the requested **Feast of Divine Mercy**. Our Lord told Sister Faustina: "This Feast emerged from my most tender pity and it is confirmed in the depths of my mercy" (Diary 420) and again, "The very depths of my tender mercy are open on that day" (Diary 699). The Polish word, translated by "depths" is literally the "Innerds or inner organs, or viscera." This is the same word that is used by our Lord to describe the source of the rays of His mercy that come from His pierced Heart: "These two rays issued forth from the very depths of My tender mercy when My agonized Heart was opened by a lance on the Cross" (Diary 299). The source of the feast of mercy and the rays of mercy are the same - the pierced Heart of Jesus, the depths of His mercy.

In the vision of the **image** of the Merciful Savior which Sister Faustina was to have painted according to the patterns she saw, Jesus points to the area of His Heart with His left hand as the source of His rays of mercy (Diary 47-49). Both in this scene and in the words of Our Lord further explaining the meaning of the rays of the image (Diary 299-300 partically quoted above), the Lord asks for the feast of mercy to be celebrated on the Sunday after Easter. It is on this feast of Divine Mercy that the rays of mercy coming from His Merciful Heart, from His very depths, like "flames of mercy" (Diary 50) are poured out on souls. The very depths of His tender mercy are open on that day - His Merciful Heart is open to all to pour out His mercy (see Diary 699).

In regard to the **Feast** of Divine Mercy, Sister writes (March 23, 1937): "Today (Tuesday of Holy Week) is the seventh day of the novena. I have received a great and inconceivable grace: the **most Merciful Heart of Jesus has promised** that I will be present at the celebration of this solemn Feast" (Diary 1042). Suddenly, she had a vision of the celebration of the feast of Divine Mercy with the Holy Father in Rome! (Diary 1044).

The Merciful Heart of Jesus as the unifying element echoes the **chaplet** of Divine Mercy in the prayer, "O Blood and Water..." which is prayed for the conversion of sinners. The sacramental elements of Blood and Water (Eucharist and Baptism) which gushed forth from the pierced Heart of Jesus are the fountain of mercy on the whole world. It is in this Jesus, with His heart opened for us, that we trust. As in the case of the Chaplet, so too, this prayer "O Blood and water..." was taught by Our Lord Himself. It is this prayer that Sister Faustina used daily to renew her self-oblation as a victim of love for souls (see Diary 309).

The Merciful Heart of Jesus is also the object of worship at the **three o'clock** hour. The hour His heart was pierced:

> At least for a moment adore in the Blessed
> Sacrament, My heart, which is full of mercy (1572).

The **Novena** before the Feast of Divine Mercy is directed to the most Compassionate Heart of Jesus. Each day Our Lord asks that a different group of people be brought to His Compassionate Heart and immersed in the ocean of His mercy (see Dairy 1209 to 1229).

It is important to see the relationship of the Merciful Heart of Jesus to the rays of Mercy, because the rays are so prominent in the message of Divine Mercy.

The Merciful Heart of Jesus is the source of the rays of mercy (Diary 87, 177, 299, 1559); specifically the pierced Heart opened by a lance for us (Diary 299, 1182, 1520) especially for sinners (Diary 1485). The red and pale rays represent-ing His Blood and Water (Diary 836, 1602) come from the depths of His tender mercy (Diary 299, 836). These rays of mercy streaming from His Merciful Heart upon the whole world (Diary 87, 836, 1559, 1689, 1796) are the source of our salvation. This wounded Heart of Jesus radiating His mer-ciful love to all is the summary and symbol of the message and devotion to the Divine Mercy.

One aspect of the **devotion** to the Merciful Heart of Jesus is described by Sister as **gazing at the Merciful Heart of Jesus:**

> My daughter, look at My Merciful Heart; I fixed my gaze at the most Sacred Heart... and understood how great is the Lord's mercy (Diary 177).

Later in her Diary, she recorded that Jesus stood before her and said:

> Look into My Heart and see there the love and mercy which I have for humankind and especially for sinners (Diary 1663).

Sister describes her retreat resolution of gazing at the Merciful Heart of Jesus:

> In difficult moments, I will fix my gaze upon the silent Heart of Jesus, stretched upon the cross, and from the exploding flames of His Merciful Heart, will flow down upon me power and strength to keep fighting (Diary 906).

Gazing on the Lord fulfills the Sacred Scriptures:

All of us, gazing with unveiled face on the glory of the Lord, are being transformed into the same image from glory to glory, as from the Lord who is the Spirit (1 Cor. 3:18).

and again:

Let us keep our eyes fixed on Jesus, who inspires and perfects our faith (Heb. 12:2).

They shall look on Him whom they have pierced (Jn 19:37).

Gazing on the Lord is the way of spirituality of the Eastern Church. They express their devotion to the Lord by standing in the presence of His Icon, gazing upon Him in reverent awe. In the Latin Church, however, the spirituality focuses more on listening to the Lord. Both gazing and listening to the Lord are the initial steps to the same goal of the union of hearts, the presence of the Lord in our hearts (see Henri Nouwen, **Gazing on the Beauty of the Lord**).

It is interesting to note that Sister Faustina gazed at the vision of the Lord Jesus depicted in the image in **silence** and awe, but also with joy (Diary 47). Silence was intregal to the union of her heart with the Heart of the Lord:

Often during Mass, I see the Lord in my soul; I feel His presence which pervades my being. I sense His divine gaze; I have long talks with Him without saying a word; I know what His Divine Heart desires, and I always do what will please Him the most (Diary 411).

And again she writes:

Amid torments I fix my eyes on You, my God... I strive for silence in my heart amidst the greatest sufferings (Diary 1040). Silence is so powerful a language that it reaches the throne of the living God.

Silence is His language, though secret, yet living and powerful (Diary 888).

In the vision of Jesus in which she is asked to gaze on His Merciful Heart, Sister is given an understanding of the greatness of His mercy (Diary 177). In the vision of Holy Thursday, 1938, quoted above she gazes at His Heart and learns more of His love for us by sharing in His passion.

Look into My Heart and see there the love and mercy which I have for mankind, and especially for sinners, and enter into My Passion. In an instant, I experienced and lived through the whole Passion of Jesus in my own heart (Diary 1663).

Then, in May of 1938, the Lord makes it clear to Sister that gazing on His Merciful Heart is a way to be formed after the pattern of His own Heart, and so, He enabled her to be merciful and proclaim His mercy to the world by having her heart set on fire with the flames of His mercy. Gazing at the Merciful Heart of Jesus sets our hearts on fire so that we can radiate His mercy:

My daughter, look into My Merciful Heart and in your own deeds, so that you, who proclaim My mercy to the world may yourself be aflame with it (Diary 1688).

Come, Holy Spirit, fill the hearts of the faithful and enkindle in them the fire of divine love. Father, send forth Your Spirit and renew the face of the earth (Proper of the Churches).

In her gazing at the Merciful Heart of Jesus, Sister Faustina lives Psalm 123:

Like the eyes of a servant on the hand of her mistress so our eyes are on the Lord our God till He shows us mercy. Have mercy, Lord, have mercy.

Sister Faustina's devotion to the Merciful Heart of Jesus was expressed by her whole mission of mercy: proclaiming His mercy by writing her "Diary", praying for souls, especially sinners, doing her daily works of mercy, offering her sufferings in union with the crucified Christ, venerating the Image of the Merciful Savior, celebrating the novena and the Feast of Divine Mercy, remembering the death of the Lord at three o'clock and praying the chaplet - placing all her trust in the Merciful Heart of Jesus (Diary 1138). But over and above these ways of honoring the Mercy of God, she records a number of ways in which she specifically honored the Merciful Heart of Jesus within her heart. Two stand out for special consideration, because of her repeated reference to them. One is hiding in the Heart of Jesus or resting on His Heart. The second is glorifying His Merciful Heart.

Like the beloved desciple who reclined at the side of Jesus at the Last Supper (see Jn 13:23), Sister Faustina, too, rested her heart on the Heart of the Lord:

> After Holy Communion, I leaned my head on the Most Sacred Heart of Jesus (Diary 1348, see also 801, 866, 929).

She would hide in the Heart of Jesus as a refuge and source of strength:

> When I see that the burden is beyond my strength, I do not consider or analyze it or probe into it, but I run like a child to the Heart of Jesus and say only one word to Him: "You can do all things. And then I keep silent..." (Diary 1033, 1621, 1629).

In the time of Satan's attacks:

> When I see His great fury, I stay inside the stronghold; that is, the most Sacred Heart of Jesus (Diary 1287).

It was at the instruction of Jesus that she took refuge in His Heart:

Do not bargain with temptation; lock yourself immediately in My Heart (Diary 1760, **Conference on Spiritual Warfare**).

Seeing her own misery and the misery of the world around her, she would "nestle close to the most Sacred Heart of Jesus" (Diary 1318, also 1327) in response to the direction of the Lord:

Tell aching mankind to snuggle close to My Merciful Heart, and I will fill it with peace (Diary 1074).

She prayed for this:

O Jesus, have mercy! Embrace the whole world and press me to Your Heart (Diary 869).

Sister wanted to glorify the Lord with every beat of her heart (see Diary 1064, 1234, 1489, 1708). She wanted to adore Him in her heart (see Diary 1385), fulfilling the exhortation of St. Peter:

Venerate the Lord, that is, Christ, in your hearts (1 Peter 3:15).

She wanted to glorify the Merciful Heart of Jesus as the mission of her life:

Oh, my Jesus, each of Your saints reflect one of Your virtues; I desire to reflect Your Compassionate Heart, full of mercy, I want to glorify it. Let Your mercy, O Jesus, be impressed upon my heart and soul like a seal, and this will be my badge in this and the future life. Glorifying Your mercy is the exclusive task of my life (Diary 1242).

She prayed that everyone would glorify the mercy of God:

> O my God, who knows every beat of my heart, You know how eagerly I desire that all hearts would beat for You alone, that every soul glorify the greatness of Your mercy (Diary 1489).

Our Lord responded to this prayer of a "perfect soul":

> I expect from you, My child, a great number of souls who will glorify My mercy for all eternity (Diary 1489).

She also prayed that she could glorify God the Father with the Merciful Heart of Jesus in a unique and special way:

> O most sweet Jesus who, in Your incomprehensible kindness, have deigned to unite my wretched heart to Your most Merciful Heart, it is with your Own Heart that I glorify God, our Father, as no soul has ever glorified Him before (Diary 836).

The gift of being able to glorify the Lord in this way she attributes to the Eucharist:

> I would not know how to give glory to God if I did not have the Eucharist in my heart (Diary 1037).

> I am praying to the living Heart of Jesus in the Blessed Sacrament... (Diary 1607).

As a way of expressing her devotion to the Merciful Heart of Jesus, she prayed addressing His Heart with the desire to have her heart transformed:

> Jesus, make my heart like unto Yours, or rather transform it into Your own Heart that I may sense the needs of other hearts, especially those who are sad and suffering. May the rays of mercy rest in my heart (Diary 514).

Jesus, make my heart like unto Your Merciful Heart
Jesus, help me to go through life doing good to everyone (Diary 692).

The devotion of Sister Faustina to the Merciful Heart of
Jesus had the goal of being united with His heart for the
sake of others, that all may glorify the mercy of God. The
Lord Jesus taught Sister clearly that the purpose of gazing
into His Merciful Heart was in order that she reflect His
mercy to the world:

> My daughter, look into My Merciful Heart and reflect
> its compassion in your own heart and in your deeds,
> so that you, who proclaim My mercy to the world,
> may yourself be aflame with it (Diary 1688).

> Be always merciful as I am merciful. Love everyone
> out of love for Me, even your enemies, so that My
> mercy may be fully reflected in your heart (Diary
> 1695).

> Tell (all people) My daughter, that I am Lord and
> Mercy itself. When a soul approaches Me with trust,
> I fill it with such an abundance of graces that it can-
> not contain them within itself, but radiates them to
> other souls (Diary 1074).

She prayed that this exposure to the radiation of Christ's
mercy would then radiate out to others:

> I expose my heart to the action of Your grace like a
> crystal exposed to the rays of the sun. May Your
> image be reflected in it, O my God, to the extent that
> it is possible to be reflected in the heart of a crea-
> ture. Let Your divinity radiate through me, O You,
> who dwell in my soul (Diary 1336).

Sister prayed in thanksgiving for God's mystery of Divine

Mercy a prayer that summarizes the devotion and message of the Merciful Heart of Jesus:

O Jesus, it is through Your most Compassionate Heart, as through a crystal, that the rays of Divine Mercy have come to us (Diary 1553).

The rays of Divine Mercy are to cover the world. At the beginning of her Diary and at the end, Sister Faustina records her vision of these rays of mercy coming from the Heart of Jesus covering the whole world:

I saw the Lord Jesus above our chapel, looking just as He did the first time I saw Him painted in the image. The two rays which emanated from the Heart of Jesus covered our chapel and the infirmary, and then the whole city, and spread out over the whole world (Diary 87, Vilnius, Oct. 26, 1934).

Then on May 8, 1938, Sister had a vision of the image raised up high on two pillars of a temple:

There was a great multitude of people, inside and outside the temple, and torrents issuing from the compassionate Heart of Jesus were flowing down upon everyone (Diary 1689).

On what can be supposed to be the Feast of the Sacred Heart (June 24, 1938) Sister recorded:

Today, I saw the Sacred Heart of Jesus in the sky, in the midst of a great brilliance. The rays were issuing from the wound (in his side) and spreading out over the entire world (Diary 1796).

In her final entry in her Diary (June 1938) she prayed:

May Your grace, which flows down upon me from Your Compassionate Heart, strengthen me for the struggle and sufferings, that I may remain faithful to You (Diary 1803).

The devotion and message of the Merciful Heart of Jesus is for everyone, not just for Sister Faustina. She records for us the words of our Lord:

Every soul, and especially the soul of every religious, should reflect My mercy. My Heart overflows with compassion and merciful for all, **the heart of My beloved must resemble Mine**; from her heart must spring the fountain of My mercy for souls; otherwise I will not acknowledge her as Mine (Diary 1148).

Everyone of us is called to resemble the Lord's Heart in its humility, purity, and love as Jesus instructed Sister Faustina (see Diary 1779) and preached to all of us:

Learn from me, for I am meek and humble of heart (Mt. 11:29).

And which He proclaimed in the Beatitude:

Blessed are the pure in heart, for they shall see God (Mt. 5:8).

which immediately follows:

Blessed are the merciful, for they shall obtain mercy (Mt. 5:7),

the great Beatitude of mercy.

The pure in heart, the single hearted, the clean of heart - as different translations render it - is the transparent purity of a crystal that allows light to enter and pass through it, allowing the heart to "see God" present in its own heart and in the hearts of others and in the fullness of time, to "see God" in all His glory.

Our Blessed Mother Mary was such a "pure heart" that she truly "saw God" in everything (Diary 1710). She asked her to "dwell with (the Lord) continually in her heart." (Diary 785), pressing Sister to her own Immaculate Heart (Diary 805, 1097, 1415), and giving peace. Sister prayed to Mary to be pure of heart (Diary 874), even like Mary's heart at the time of the annunciation (Diary 1114).

Sister Faustina prayed that the rays of mercy would purify her heart:

> O sweet rays of God, enlighten me to the secret depth, for I want to arrive at the greatest possible purity of heart and soul (Diary 852).

Devotion to the Merciful Heart of Jesus is special. It is the summary of all the devotions, unifying them in the very person of Jesus - in His divine - human Heart which is mercy itself.

Like Sister Faustina, we too, are to gaze on the Merciful Heart of Jesus and be irradiated by the rays of His mercy, transformed by them to be pure of heart, and so radiate His mercy to all - that all may glorify His mercy.

> For Jesus is our Hope; through His Merciful Heart, as through an open gate we pass through to heaven (Diary 1570).